HEADLINES FROM THE FIRST THREE YEARS

 **VERA BAIRD**
POLICE & CRIME COMMISSIONER

Foreword by Rt Hon Harriet Harman QC MP

Published by: pinkapublishing

Copyright ©: Office of the Police and Crime Commissioner

ISBN: 978-1-5262-0002-0

November 2015

HEADLINES FROM THE FIRST THREE YEARS

VERA BAIRD
POLICE & CRIME COMMISSIONER

CONTENTS

08
INTRODUCTION

12
FOREWORD

16
THANKS TO SUPPORT AGENCIES

20
SECTION 1
VIOLENCE AGAINST WOMEN AND GIRLS

- 22 SAFEGUARDING IN THE NIGHT
- 28 WHEN IS RAPE NOT A RAPE?
- 38 PROJECT MIRABAL: TAKING A LEAD AGAINST DOMESTIC VIOLENCE PERPETRATORS
- 48 WORKPLACES UNITE TO TACKLE DOMESTIC AND SEXUAL ABUSE
- 54 DVSA CARS: A NEW SERVICE FOR DOMESTIC VIOLENCE VICTIMS

62
SECTION 2
IMPROVING THE CRIMINAL JUSTICE SYSTEM

- PUTTING VICTIMS FIRST
- CHANGING POLICE CULTURE BY POSITIVELY HANDLING COMPLAINTS
- SEEING IS BELIEVING: NORTHUMBRIA'S COURT OBSERVERS
- THE FIRST TRIAL: COURT OBSERVERS TELL THE STORY
- PROJECT SANCTUARY: TARGETING SEXUAL EXPLOITATION AND WORKING WITH OTHERS TO PROTECT THE VULNERABLE
- PROGRESS AGAINST DOMESTIC ABUSE THROUGH UNDERSTANDING COERCIVE CONTROL
- WE NEED OUR HUMAN RIGHTS – DISPELLING THE MYTHS
- FIGHTING FOR FAIR FUNDING FROM GOVERNMENT

130
SECTION 3
THE ROLE OF THE POLICE AND CRIME COMMISSIONER

- 132 THE ROLE OF THE POLICE AND CRIME COMMISSIONER

INTRODUCTION

In November 2015 it will be three years since my election as Labour Police and Crime Commissioner for Northumbria. I wanted to write about some of the work we have been doing on behalf of the public, aspects of which, pleasingly and excitingly, are being taken up by others and might even blaze a small trail nationally.

The articles I have written will show that almost everything is done in partnership with a cross section of agencies - private, public, voluntary, community and charitable - as well as through our key working relationship with Northumbria Police. Though some of the articles refer to legal ideas or concepts I have tried to write them in accessible language; not easy for a lawyer. They are organised in three sections: Violence against Women and Girls; Improving the Criminal Justice System and The role of the Police and Crime Commissioner.

In all of this work I have taken my lead from the Northumbria public. Public consultation shaped the Police and Crime Plan (2013 – 2018) and the police deliver that plan now as their main task. Although the Police and Crime Plan will continue to evolve, the public have made clear that the priorities we set in 2013 are just as important today.

You can find out much more about our work and our plan on the website www.northumbria-pcc.gov.uk.

The services my team and I provide cost almost £3m LESS than the former Police Authority; these savings have gone back into policing and community safety. The next few years will be even more challenging than the previous three, with further massive budget reductions, but neighbourhood policing will continue to be a priority since, wherever I go, people tell me how much they value their contact with their local police and staff teams.

The articles included here are about the impact, both locally and on public policy too, of headline work in our first three years. Some of the schemes are new and therefore still 'work in progress', but I wanted to share with you my enthusiasm for what has been achieved so far. We think that here in the North East, we are helping to shape public policy across England and Wales as well as in practical ways bringing change and improved well-being to our local community.

Vera Baird QC
Police & Crime Commissioner – Northumbria

FOREWORD

'Headlines From the First Three Years' captures the profound difference Vera Baird QC has made as the Police and Crime Commissioner for Northumbria proving to be a strong voice for local residents and a driving force for cultural changes.

If the North East is to continue to redevelop its commercial and industrial strength and to thrive economically it is vital that it continues to be a safe place to live. The responsibility for that is, of course, far broader than ensuring effective local policing, although that is key. It also involves good preventative and intervention policies in which local partners come together to share resources and work jointly. Supporting victims to help them to cope and recover from crime is as fundamental as backing diversionary projects to direct young people into positive activities. It is also vital to support an efficient and effective Criminal Justice System. Northumbria benefits in all of these areas, from a Police and Crime Commissioner with wide experience as a criminal law QC, with an understanding not only of the core Criminal Justice System, but also about policing and the prime importance of civil liberties and human rights.

When in Parliament as a Labour MP, Vera fought for better rights for victims of domestic abuse and for justice for women who killed their violent partners and additionally showed her understanding of needs beyond those of the justice system when she led debates on pension rights and housing. As Solicitor General, she helped me take the Equality Act 2010 through its Parliamentary stages and is as committed as I am to the sense of fairness that underpins that law. Her executive experience as a Departmental Minister has no doubt helped her to make the landmark savings in office costs alone of over £3m with all savings reinvested back into policing.

The wheels of justice are known to work slowly but in Northumbria, in three short years, some of the changes set out here have begun to make a difference.

The first ever Court Observers Panel, staffed by trained volunteers has already reported findings to the judiciary and the prosecution authorities who have responded positively. Victims First Northumbria, the ground-breaking hub has, since its inception in April, supported many victims of crime referred by police and many who needed support but did not want police involvement. The scores of businesses and public authorities who have adopted Workplace Domestic and Sexual Abuse Policies and put Champions in place to support victims of abuse who seek help at work are testimony to the sound partnerships that have responded to Vera's lead in this critical area.

The priorities in the Police and Crime Plan were set by the public and are at the core of delivery by Northumbria Police, a high-performing force, popular with the public and embedded into the communities through a strong focus on neighbourhood policing.

This book gives an insight into achievements so far and a glimmer of the exciting work yet to come from Northumbria under the leadership of Vera Baird, the Police and Crime Commissioner.

Rt Hon Harriet Harman QC MP

THANKS TO SUPPORT AGENCIES

In drawing up these new public policy initiatives the Office of the Police and Crime Commissioner for Northumbria has worked with a number of agencies in the public, private, voluntary and community, and charitable sectors.

I and my team would like to thank:

Ahmed Khan Restaurant Ltd
Aone - Road Asset Management
Barnardo's
Beecham and Peacock Solicitors
Blyth Resource and Initiative Centre - Community Hub.
British Telecom
British Transport Police
Creative Support - Gateshead, Sunderland
Dicksons Family Pork Butchers
G4S Utilities
Gateshead Carers
Gateshead College
Gateshead Council
GE Gas and Oil
Gentoo
GMB - Union
Gordon Brown, Law firm
Helen McCardle Care - Gateshead, Durham, Newcastle
Her Majesty Courts and Tribunal Services
HM Revenue and Customs

Her Majesty's Prison Service
Holmes Stroud
Home Group
Home Secretary, Rt Hon Theresa May MP
HOPE Consortium - Newcastle
Impact Family Services
Institute of Directors - Professional
Institute of Directors.
International Paint Ltd
Intu - Metro centre and Eldon Square
Muckle LLP - Commercial Law Firm
Newcastle City Council
Newcastle College
Newcastle/Gateshead Initiative - Local event information site
NHS Business Service Authority - Local and National
North East Ambulance Service
North East Chamber of Commerce
North Tyneside Council
Northridge Care Ltd
Northumberland County Council
Northumberland Recovery Partnership - Recovery Centre
Oasis Aquilla - Supported Housing
Phoenix Security
Places for People
Primark - Metro Centre
Respect
Ringtons - Local and National
Soroptimists - Newcastle Branch
South Tyneside Council
St John's Ambulance
Stage Coach
Sunderland Council
Tesco - Gateshead, North Tyneside, Northumberland, South Tyneside
The Security Industry Authority
Tyne and Wear Fire Service
Tyneside Rape Crisis
Unison
UNITE
Victims First Northumbria
Ward Hadaway - Law Firm
Wearside Women in Need
West End Women and Girls
Winn Solicitors

Your Homes Newcastle

Finally, I want to thank the hugely supportive staff of the OPCC and my co-authors Clare Phillipson and Chief Constable Steve Ashman and particular gratitude for the input and advice of Boni Sones OBE.

01 SAFEGUARDING IN THE NIGHT

02 WHEN IS RAPE NOT A RAPE?

03 PROJECT MIRABAL: TAKING A LEAD AGAINST DOMESTIC VIOLENCE PERPETRATORS

04 WORKPLACES UNITE TO TACKLE DOMESTIC AND SEXUAL ABUSE

05 DVSA CARS: A NEW SERVICE FOR DOMESTIC VIOLENCE VICTIMS

SECTION 1

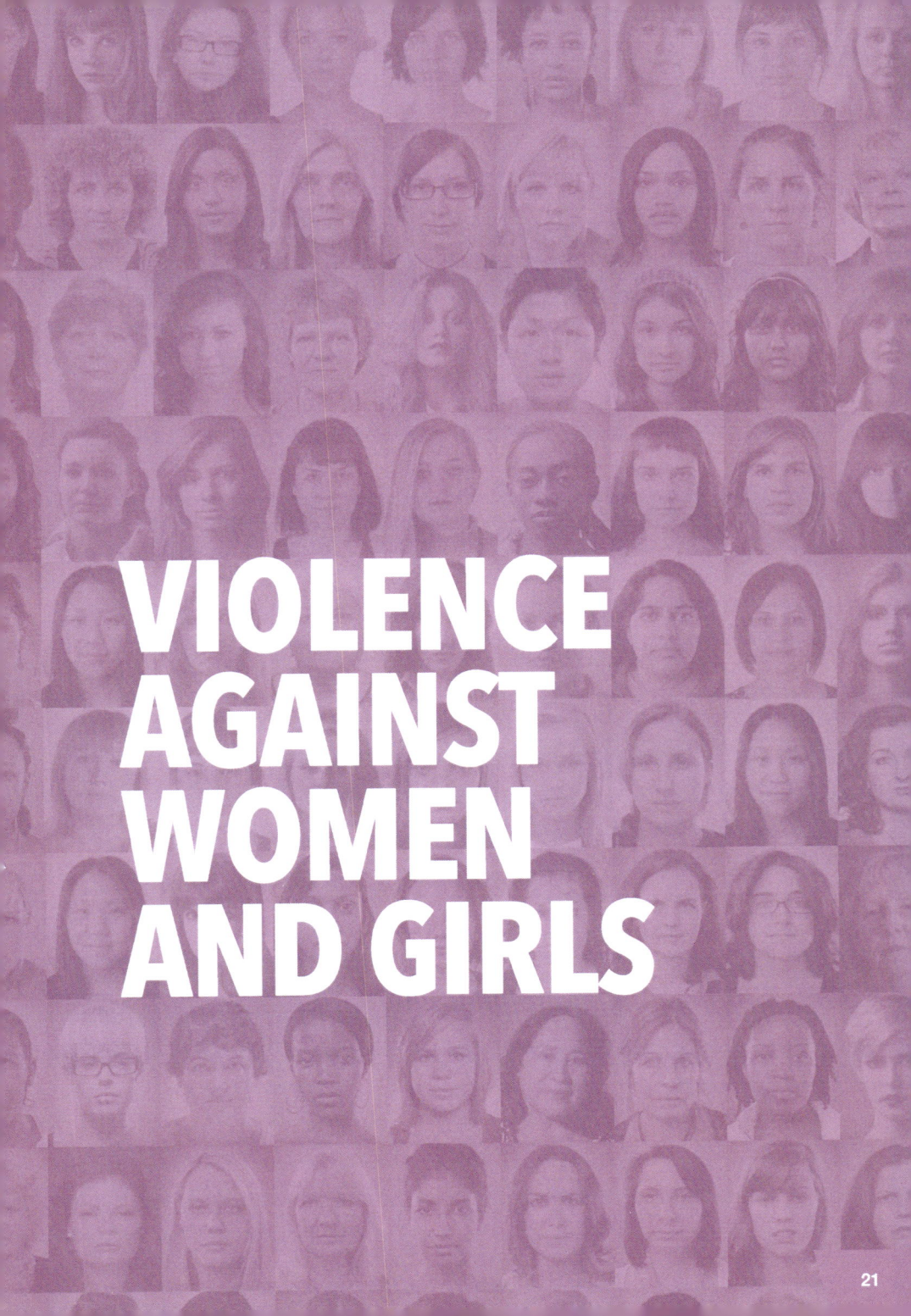

VIOLENCE AGAINST WOMEN AND GIRLS

"In Northumbria, by training door staff, street pastors, hotel staff, transport workers and British Transport Police, our cities are acquiring more 'eyes and ears' available and alert to keeping people safer."

01
SAFEGUARDING IN THE NIGHT

Women, like men get drunk, but lighter body weight and an equal sense of being part of the crowd of peers male and female, might mean they more easily tip over a threshold. Police nationwide know that predatory men hang around every night-time economy looking for just that vulnerability – easy prey and, the criminals believe, a victim who is likely to be too chaotic or too ashamed to tell the authorities and too unreliable for police action if they do.

In Newcastle in 2013, there was a devastating multiple rape of a 17 year old girl who was excluded from a popular city centre club after becoming very intoxicated. She had lost her friends and the doorman walked her towards a taxi rank but with such difficulty that he accepted help from a male passer-by. A couple of taxis refused to take her and the doorman, anxious to go back to work, left her with the male. He immediately had sex with her in a corner and then passed her on to two other men, who took her around the city, sometimes carrying her, and having sex with her for four or five hours. She finally 'came to' in a car park with someone on top of her and fled to a club where a couple called the police. Officers were able to assemble the events of the night from the city's extensive CCTV coverage and two of the three men were arrested, charged with rape and received substantial sentences.

The shocking persistence with which they had toted her round for hours appeared to forestall any victim-blaming against her and was so disturbing that it demanded a new approach to dealing with people when they are vulnerable through drink.

The problem started with the club doorman who saw his role as protecting a single set of premises from trouble, with no thought of what might befall the young woman once she had been removed. He was not untypical. We were to find that there was no element of safeguarding training in the Security Industry Authority's door-staff qualifications and no reference to any duty of care to the public at large. Such a narrow view of the role meant that the staff had no training about predatory men, as was quite clear from the attitude of the doorman in question, when he let the rapist take the girl away.

There was also an issue for the police because two members of the public had complained to passing officers when they saw the first assailant having sex with the victim in a corner but he persuaded them that they were a couple, an assertion reinforced because she was clinging to his neck. However, she was hardly able to stand and could barely speak and the officers should have known that the law makes clear that sex with a woman who is so drunk that she cannot consent is rape.

There are 57,000 students in Newcastle who, with thousands of other young people, enjoy the extensive nightlife. Indeed, it is a part of the pull used by North East universities to attract students. It has been a very safe place, thanks to street pastors, positive policing and a number of poster campaigns to encourage people to keep themselves safe such as one declaring: 'Keys, Money, Phone, Plans to Get Home'.

Following this case, all the responsible agencies in the city understood that they had to do more to keep young people safer, to safeguard the city's reputation and that the public needed reassurance and so needed to play a part.

Police and Crime Commissioners are the public's voice in policing and they have a role, with community safety partners to help to prevent crime. In both capacities I joined the city Police Superintendent, licensing, adult services and community safety staff from the council, and representatives from health services, probation and the business community and asked them to work with me and the Tyneside Rape Crisis Centre so that we could work out, from every viewpoint, what needed to be done.

Originally the police were uncritical of their officers' behaviour and made the cogent point that they couldn't interview every couple they saw in the city centre because the female was drunk. However, police have a duty to prevent crime and neither officer seemed to have understood or applied the legal principle that she would have been too drunk to be capable of consenting to sex. We involved Tyneside Rape Crisis, who are as well-versed as the police in the working methods of predatory men, and together they developed a 'core conversation' which means that officers will now separate the alleged couple, ask key questions and compare the answers to ascertain whether they believe that they should intervene to protect someone the worse for drink from being hijacked for sexual abuse.

The door-staff training package teaches how to assess an individual's vulnerability, whether through alcohol, having lost contact with friends, being upset or confused, wet or cold or having ended up in an environment known to be risky. An important aspect of the new training was a switch in understanding that a supervisor's role is not confined to his or her employer's property but extends to a duty to care for everyone with whom they come into contact. Rather than excluding or refusing entry to someone who is assessed as vulnerable, door staff will now invite them into a quiet place on the premises and try to assure their safety. This scheme was strongly supported by Phoenix Security, a key supplier of door staff in the North East.

The police donated an adapted vehicle, called the Safe Haven which is parked at night, in the city centre with a St John's ambulance vehicle. Both will take in anyone who is in need of help or support. Door-staff, street pastors and police can all take vulnerable people there and the cost of both vehicles is more than recovered from savings on ambulance call-outs and trips to accident and emergency. 'Drunk tanks' which keep people overnight, charge for admission and result in a police penalty notice, are not part of our strategy. We see those consequences of seeking help as a heavy deterrent to people seeking help for themselves or a needy friend and we intend to prioritise keeping the vulnerable safe.

This work has brought local police and door-staff into a better working relationship. Police generally consider pubs and clubs who call them out at night to be nuisance premises but they now appreciate that calls about safeguarding show a positive attitude, likelier from a well-run business. They welcome door staff intervening to help people whereas before, it is said, that they regarded public places as police-only territory.

I went on one of the training courses and door-staff told me that they had seen incidents outside their premises in the past and not known whether they should intervene. They now felt empowered to help and touchingly, asked for a lapel badge to wear on duty. All trained door staff in Newcastle can now wear a metal badge showing a pair of hands holding the words 'Safe Haven'.

The Security Industry Authority has significantly professionalised door supervision, in recent years, bringing a sometime disreputable business into respectability and reliability. They are responsible for training and accreditation and overall are accountable to the Home Office.

I met with the Home Secretary. Theresa May, and asked if she was aware that there was no safeguarding component in training and told her the story of the young woman in Newcastle. The combination of her support and the Security Industry Authority's keenness to continue to progress the door supervisor role culminated in the Authority adopting our training as a matter of urgency. By September of 2013, the Northumbria Safeguarding Course was a compulsory module in the initial training for door supervisors. Nobody can qualify as a door supervisor now without taking our course so that city by city and town by town over 100,000 door staff in the UK are acquiring the safeguarding skills which everyone would want to have available to keep members of their family safe on an evening out.

There is plenty of anecdotal feedback on an innovation that would not be easy formally to evaluate. One woman was seen wandering on her own, late in the night, and somewhat the worse for wear. A supervisor spoke to her, although she had not been in his premises and offered to help her to find her friends or family. He suggested she waited while he contacted police and they, in turn, were able to find a friend to take her home.

On another occasion an intoxicated young woman was walking along with two men whose demeanour caused a doorman to be concerned.

He asked if she was with the men. She said she didn't know them and the supervisor asked them why they were hanging around her. The men started to look uncomfortable, so he invited the woman in and called the police who spoke to the men while she was taken home in a taxi.

A young woman, somewhat the worse for drink and wending her way along Newcastle's Collingwood Street, was approached by a doorman and invited to take a seat in the entrance of his club. He brought her some water. She had lost her friends and couldn't easily have got home but the doorman found that her mobile phone book held an entry 'Mum and Dad' and with her permission, he rang for her parents. Her father arrived shortly afterwards and the following day emailed me, in a very touching way, saying how grateful they were for our work in protecting his daughter against what could have been disastrous events.

We have offered the police training to all the Police and Crime Commissioners in England and Wales and many are taking it on. In Northumbria, we have trained our street pastors, hotel staff, transport workers and British Transport Police, so that our cities are acquiring more 'eyes and ears' available and alert to keeping people safer, a positive legacy from that terrible rape.

"It seems at last possible that prejudiced and slipshod attitudes to rape complainants might, perforce, soon be made as unacceptable in the police as they have been for many years to rape campaigners."

02
WHEN IS RAPE NOT A RAPE?

Some Northumbria Police officers decided that 33 of the 168 rapes reported to them in 2014 were 'no-crimes' meaning no offence had happened and the law had not been broken at all. Her Majesty's Inspectors of Constabulary reviewing a sample of those cases did not agree and neither did I, having read every one, as the local Police and Crime Commissioner.

In total 11 of the 'no-crimes' gave cause for serious concerns. Consequently a number of police officers were moved to other duties and a senior officer has been appointed by the Chief Constable to investigate whether these 'no-rapes' may have been rapes after all.

Every report of rape should be recorded, within 24 hours, and then investigated. Occasionally with all crimes, the investigation shows that no offence has been committed. Home Office counting rules could not be clearer that a 'no-crime' designation means that the allegation was not in fact a crime, either because it has been incorrectly recorded as one, or because there is 'additional verifiable evidence' to show that it did not take place.

However, some Northumbria rape cases were 'no-crimed' because the woman was extremely drunk and the man said she'd consented. The law says: 'If the complainant becomes so intoxicated that she no longer has the capacity to agree, there will be no consent' (R v Bree 2007 EWCA 256). Taking sexual advantage of someone who is mindlessly drunk, apart from being an appalling abuse of another person, can, therefore, be the crime of rape. It should not be 'no-crimed'. It is also not the job of a police officer to decide that she probably consented because she was drunk, still less that she let herself become 'fair game' by drinking.

Incredibly too, officers decided, in some cases, that there was 'additional verifiable evidence' showing a rape complaint to be a no-crime because the defendant denied it or claimed consent. Other cases were also found to match campaigners' views of the myths and stereotypes that still obfuscate clear consideration of rape throughout the justice system. For instance, partner rape was sometimes 'no-crimed' even though the complainant said she did not consent, seemingly because she had consented to sex with him both before and since. Such views return us to the days when rape in marriage was literally not a crime; when the law itself failed to recognise that marrying someone did not mean that a woman had given unlimited and unconditional consent to sex. Another group of cases were just very worrying mysteries; where the complainant told the police in compelling detail, sometimes supported by injuries, how she was raped and the next day a retraction statement was added to the file, saying that she now agreed that she wasn't.

It is not up to the police to decide that in their experience this is the kind of rape case that never gets to court or won't bring a conviction and so it should be abandoned at the outset. The Administrative Court criticised just such an approach when taken by the Crown Prosecution Service as a reason not to prosecute (*www.bailii.org/ew/ cases/EWHC/Admin/2009/106.html*). Lord Justice Toulson acknowledged that in cases where convictions are hard to obtain, including some rapes:

"If (the decision-maker) were to apply a purely predictive approach, based on past experience of similar cases (the bookmaker's approach) he might well feel unable to conclude that a jury was more likely than not to convict the defendant".

But, he said, such an approach would be mere 'statistical guess work' which the authorities should avoid, instead adopting a 'merits based approach' in which the prosecutor imagines him/herself

to be the fact finder and asks whether the evidence is sufficient to merit a conviction.

Clearly if cases are rejected on 'the bookmaker's approach' because similar ones have failed, no effort will ever be made to improve how those cases are dealt with and to increase the conviction rate and there will be, as Lord Justice Toulson said in the Crown Prosecution Service case, categories of complainants who never get justice.

Incorrect 'no-criming' of rape is not a new problem and it is not confined to Northumbria Police officers. In 2002 Her Majesty's Inspectorate of Constabulary and Crown Prosecution Service Inspectorate found that 31.8% of sampled rape cases that had been 'no-crimed' had been no-crimed wrongly, and also found in 2005-6 that of 179 rapes 'no-crimed' 57 were wrong. *www.justiceinspectorates. gov.uk/hmic/media/without-consent-20061231.pdf*

In 2012 in a further report, called 'Forging the Links', *www. justiceinspectorates.gov.uk/hmic/ publications/forging-the-links-rape-investigation-and-prosecution* both inspectorates also found that 2,131 rape offences had been 'no-crimed', in the previous year, nearly 12% of all recorded rapes,

with wild variation from 2.4% to 30% across forces. In contrast, only 3% of recorded offences of causing grievous bodily harm with intent were 'no-crimed' though this is a similarly serious offence and recorded in similar numbers to rape. Samples of 'no-crimed' rapes, in that year, showed that 11% of them were wrong.

Believing that a case won't get to court or secure a conviction is not the only problematic assumption brought to bear by Crown Prosecution Service lawyers and police officers however; the latter may also decide that an allegation is false, even when there is little if any evidence to support such a view.

In 2005, for example, the Home Office commissioned in-depth research called: 'A Gap or a Chasm: Attrition in Reported Rape Cases'- *webarchive.nationalarchives.gov. uk/20110218135832/rds.homeoffice. gov.uk/rds/pdfs05/hors293.pdf*. This looked at a sample of 'no-crimes' deemed by police to be false allegations. In about a third of the sample, police said that the complainant had admitted to its falsity, a fifth had decided not to proceed, a handful did not co-operate and in the remainder of cases the decision was made by the police on evidential grounds. On the researchers' analysis, however, only about a third of those cases were either probably or possibly false and when they spoke to officers on this topic they found that:

"Even if the complaints originally designated as false were really all false (approximately 10%) that was still a much lower number of false complaints than the officers they interviewed perceived to be normal".

Recognising that the individual and collective perceptions of police officers were therefore likely to be crucial, the researchers then pursued how police officers went about assessing truth and falsity in allegations concluding that there was:

"A culture of suspicion … even amongst some of those who are specialists in rape investigations [and a] tendency to conflate false allegations with retractions and withdrawals, as if in all such cases no sexual assault occurred".

Every piece of research on this topic shows that police officers habitually over-estimate the number of false rape allegations, perhaps because categorising false allegations and withdrawn or retracted allegations as 'no-crimes' means that the two are seen as the same. This creates a circular process where officers decide a case is doomed, on Lord Justice Toulson's 'bookmakers approach' and wrongly 'no-crime' it, thereby adding to the incorrect but widespread police belief that there are high levels of false complaints and, in turn, encouraging cavalier treatment of similar cases in the future.

Baroness Stern in her review in 2010 *webarchive.nationalarchives. gov.uk/20110608160754/http:/ www.equalities.gov.uk/PDF/Stern_ Review_acc_FINAL.pdf* thought the issue of false complaints was so contested that the Ministry of Justice ought to ascertain its true extent. The Crown Prosecution Service also tackled the issue in 2013, with the Director of Public Prosecutions considering every would-be false allegation personally for 17 months. In total, just 35 cases were prosecuted; a tiny number compared to the 5651 rape prosecutions that took place in the same time period.

In 2015, Professor Betsy Stanko was given a large, representative sample of rape complaints made to the Metropolitan Police. She was considering attrition between report and court, in which 'no-criming' plays a part and noted that attrition is at its highest level early in an investigation so that the police have a dual role '…to investigate the complaint, and since in rape the

victim is usually the key witness, to keep the victim engaged in the criminal justice process'.

And yet, 48% of the cases which failed at an early stage did so because of victim withdrawals; an outcome which led to many cases being categorised as 'false allegations' but which Stanko attributed to the behaviour of police officers and to the important finding that:

"The tentative trust required to report the rape is lost when police officers communicate disbelief and disrespect".

It seems that officers, over-ready to categorise withdrawals as false allegations, transmit their scepticism to the complainant, and lose their trust. For example, 19% of cases lost early were 'no-crimed'. If the police record showed a previous 'false allegation' by the victim the odds of 'no-criming' increased by 786%, although a 'false allegation' could be anything, as the research shows, from her own decision to withdraw to an earlier 'no-crime' because she was drunk or married to the suspect. Evidence casting doubt on her allegation increased the odds of 'no-criming' by 585% but even where there was no such evidence, a police officer expressing doubt about what she said increased the odds of 'no-criming' by 240%.

"The most influential factor" the researchers concluded, "is the perceived credibility of the allegation in light of the evidence as seen through the eyes of the investigating police officer and prosecutor" - 'Complaints of Rape and the Criminal Justice System, Fresh evidence on the attrition problem' *euc.sagepub.com/content/early/2015/02/27/1477370815571949.abstract*; a finding that has been highlighted by multiple research studies and which quantities of policies have, thus far, failed to address.

However, recent developments may generate fresh hope.

Firstly, the action that Northumbria Police has taken is very strong and could easily set the future benchmark for other forces. A senior investigating officer has been appointed under the direct command of the Chief Constable to review every 'no-crimed' rape and to investigate whether professional misconduct was involved in its initial handling. A large number of senior police in a key specialist department have been put at risk of disciplinary action, which has operated like an earthquake in the force. Such action was imperative, in the context of Rotherham and many other cases where allegations of 'turning a blind eye' to exploitative sex cases has put senior officers at risk, viz, the recent Independent Police Complaints Commission investigation into such allegations against the Chief Constable of Greater Manchester.

In addition to disciplinary action, there must be an additional risk of criminal prosecution for misconduct in a public office by wilfully neglecting the duty to investigate a serious offence. This could be levelled against investigating officers, supervision or command ranks and has been brought to the fore, together with a serious risk of civil damages, by the recent High Court case about John Worboys. He was the London taxi driver who raped about 195 women by systematically drugging them when they were his passengers. The case determined that the police have a duty to victims to investigate, independently and impartially, whenever there is 'a credible arguable claim' of an offence. It is an aspect of the state's duty to protect citizens from inhuman and degrading treatment under the Human Rights Act and Article 3 of the European Convention. The Metropolitan Police were in breach of that duty to two of Worboys' victims which, the Court said, had compounded their trauma whilst allowing Worboys to continue to rape. (DSD v Commissioner of Police for the Metropolis 2014 EWHC 436) Certainly, 'no-criming' 'a credible arguable claim' of rape without any independently verifiable evidence would be a similar breach of duty.

Further, the appointment of the first non-police officer to the role of HM Inspector of Constabulary has brought more civilians into the inspectorate. Only a minority of inspectors are now ex-police, with the majority from civilian backgrounds in the Audit Commission and the Crown Prosecution Service. Although most of the wider staff team are still ex-police or temporary secondees, this civilianisation has brought the inspectorate closer to a citizen's vantage point, demonstrated in particular by the vigour with which Her Majesty's Inspectorate of Constabulary confronted poor domestic abuse policing and drove change in this related area of practice.

Added to that, elected Police and Crime Commissioners are in post with the statutory obligation to scrutinise police on behalf of the public. This is a new source of intense scrutiny on controversial policing issues like rape. In

Northumbria, as in many other areas, domestic and sexual abuse are key public priorities which the Commissioner can compel the police to tackle. Having the budget in the hands of an elected civilian is a significant, if little appreciated, shift of power away from police and towards the public.

I personally read all Northumbria's controversial 'no-crimed' rapes without knowing that similarly, Professor Stanko was reading police files 300 miles away in the Metropolitan Police. Unlike hers my findings are not of statistical significance, but they are essentially the same.

In one Northumbria case a woman showed the police injuries compatible with her account and yet was given her clothes back the next day and told she hadn't been raped. The file showed no other cause for her injuries. The rape, in a park, of a woman with learning difficulties was 'no-crimed' because she just asked police to take her home and didn't make an immediate complaint - even though a witness saw the sex she later talked about taking place. Officers in these cases face misconduct notices and in separate cases, two alleged rapists face prosecution in Newcastle Crown Court for allegations that were originally 'no-crimed'.

It seems at last possible that prejudiced and slipshod attitudes to rape complainants might, perforce, soon be made as unacceptable in the police as they have been for many years to rape campaigners. One of the victims in the Rotherham abuse scandal describes how police were looking at her and at what was wrong with her and not listening to what she said. There is no doubt that senior officers who do not ensure that such an attitude disappears from policing will be vulnerable, from now on, to misconduct allegations, possible prosecution and civil damages, due to the clear principles set out in the Worboys case, the refreshed approach of Her Majesty's Inspectorate of Constabulary and the local clout of the elected Police and Crime Commissioner.

"As a trustee of Respect I am pleased to be at the forefront of building on the rock of the Mirabal Project and the organisations long-lived accreditation expertise."

03
PROJECT MIRABAL: TAKING A LEAD AGAINST DOMESTIC VIOLENCE PERPETRATORS

> We have to change the behaviour of perpetrators of domestic abuse or we will be perpetually picking up the pieces of the women's lives they have damaged. It is long overdue that there was a well-informed and determined drive in this direction and Northumbria Police and its partners are taking a lead.

Since the 1970s the feminist movement has campaigned to gain recognition of the problem of domestic violence and to get resources to help women and girls who are victims. The refuge movement, Women's Aid, the rape crisis sector and, more recently campaigns against honour based abuse have all evolved along that model, commendably, giving impetus to the issue, and gaining it profile.

It is not surprising that equal energy and resource has not been applied to changing the behaviour of perpetrators of abuse. It looks like a low priority compared to safeguarding victims and children, and should be the Criminal Justice System's business, not that of women's rights campaigners. Indeed for parts of the women's movement, the concept of 'working with men' would not have been on the agenda.

There have been attempts, nonetheless, to frame programmes to help. In the 1980s the American Duluth Model of a co-ordinated community response recognised the need for action to deal with males who were not imprisoned for domestic abuse and, in the UK, Domestic Violence Perpetrator Programmes developed. These are mainly voluntary and community sector run group-work programmes, based on a gendered analysis and influenced by a diversity of practice. They developed flexibly, led by a National Practitioner's Network which started the membership organisation, Respect, in 2001 to accredit similar programmes. *(respect.uk.net)*. However, Domestic Violence Perpetrator Programmes struggled to establish their legitimacy and initial support from the probation service was withdrawn in 2005 when it developed its own Integrated Domestic Abuse Programme said to be more responsive, delivered by more skilled staff and with more robust women's support. The National Offender Management Service has now replaced Integrated Domestic Abuse Programme with the Building Better Relationships Programme, which is said to have a less gendered analysis, though there is a lack of transparency about the programme and its evaluation, presumably because it will be marketed by the new commercially run Community Rehabilitation Companies. This has all led to a separation from the voluntary and community sector, at least of court-mandated programmes, and Domestic Violence Perpetrator Programmes have refocused onto the family courts, risk assessment work, and closer work with local authority children's services.[1]

This diversity of programmes for different purposes, some of them mandated by a range of courts and some voluntary, has led to a lack of clarity as to referral criteria and some mutual distrust amongst deliverers and has given rise to a confusion about what, if anything, is available for whom and what works.

There has not been coherent or systematic development of this aspect of tackling domestic abuse on anything like the scale necessary for perpetrator change to become an automatic and accessible consequence when abuse is taking place. Clearly the Criminal Justice System has to play a part by using more Building Better Relationships programmes and prison-based perpetrator work but relatively few cases get into the Criminal Justice System at all.

---

[1] This history is drawn with gratitude from - Phillips, R., Kelly, L. and Westmarland, N. (2013). Domestic violence perpetrator programmes: an historical overview. London and Durham: London Metropolitan University and Durham University.

Figures from Northumbria Police, typical of the national picture, show how limited the role of the Criminal Justice System is in resolving domestic abuse. Firstly, fewer than a quarter of domestic abuse victims anywhere, ever complain to the police, so the vast majority never engage with the justice system at all. Of those that do, the figures show a low conversion rate from incident to conviction.

In Northumbria, there were 27,275 domestic abuse complaints in 2013 but only 4,355 crimes were recorded. This is partly because officers have limited options if victims don't want to co-operate with a charge against the perpetrator, but there are still concerns, in some force areas, about how police respond to calls about domestic violence. A report in 2014, by Her Majesty's Inspectorate of Constabulary called 'Everybody's Business' was deeply critical of all but half a dozen forces, finding a lack of visible leadership, 'alarming and unacceptable weaknesses in core policing activity in particular the collection of evidence' and a lack of 'skills and knowledge necessary to engage confidently and competently with victims of domestic abuse'.

All forces were required to produce an action plan and the whole agenda has been driven strongly through a National Oversight Group chaired by the Home Secretary. It is very likely that re-inspection this year will show significant improvement, boosted by widespread adoption of body worn video cameras so that officers collect live evidence as they go along. Victims groups say that if police do respond more effectively, there will be an increase in victims who are willing to go to court. Even so, many victims are likely still only to call the police for emergency help and not go on to pursue a criminal justice outcome. When cases do get to court, sentencing focuses on punishing the level of violence used and rarely on the need to change a course of conduct. All in all therefore, there is a clear need for a different route in addition to the Criminal Justice System if we are to make real headway in changing perpetrators behaviour.

A precursor to making a step change is to understand what confidence can be placed in which kinds of perpetrator programmes and a clear understanding of what they can achieve.

Last January (2015) saw publication of the Project Mirabal report, an independent research project into the effectiveness of

Respect accredited Domestic Violence Perpetrator Programmes[2] which can be available in the community, irrespective of criminal justice outcomes. The headline results are strong and challenge us to leave scepticism behind and develop new programmes. It was a full five year evaluation of Domestic Violence Perpetrator Programmes, the most extensive ever done in the UK and it established that the vast majority of men who abuse their partners stop physical and sexual violence if they attend a Respect accredited Domestic Violence Perpetrator Programmes.

Before attending, a third of these men had made their women partners do something sexual they did not want to do, but none of the participants did so again after taking part in the programme. Cases of men using a weapon against their partner reduced from 29% to zero. Far fewer women reported being physically injured after the programme, from 61% to 2%. And over half of the women reported feeling 'very safe' after the programme, compared to less than one in ten before (51% compared to 8%), with those feeling 'not safe at all' down from 32% to 6%.

These improvements last, but only develop after significant time within the programmes. It emerged that one of the reasons perpetrators are abusive is because they hold particular ideas about masculinity and gender roles, which take consistent, time-consuming effort to challenge.

One of the men interviewed said:

"It's never like this light bulb moment. It's like this little coin that you drop in and it bounces around for ages and it sort of argues with yourself and all of a sudden – Dink! - it's in the bottom before you know it".

Some of the results around changing non-violent coercive behaviour were weaker, though almost all showed some improvement. There was only a 2% increase in women who answered positively the question whether their partner now "behaved in a considerate manner". Using money or finances to control a partner was still a feature, although trying to prevent partners from seeing friends or family - another typical aspect of controlling behaviour - went down from 65% to 15%, with the same reduction in partners telling women how to dress. Providers of these programmes and

---

[2] Kelly, L. and Westmarland, N (2015) Domestic Violence Perpetrator Programmes: Steps Towards Change. Project Mirabal: London University and Durham University Final Report and other Mirabal documents available at www.dur.ac.uk/criva/projectmirabal

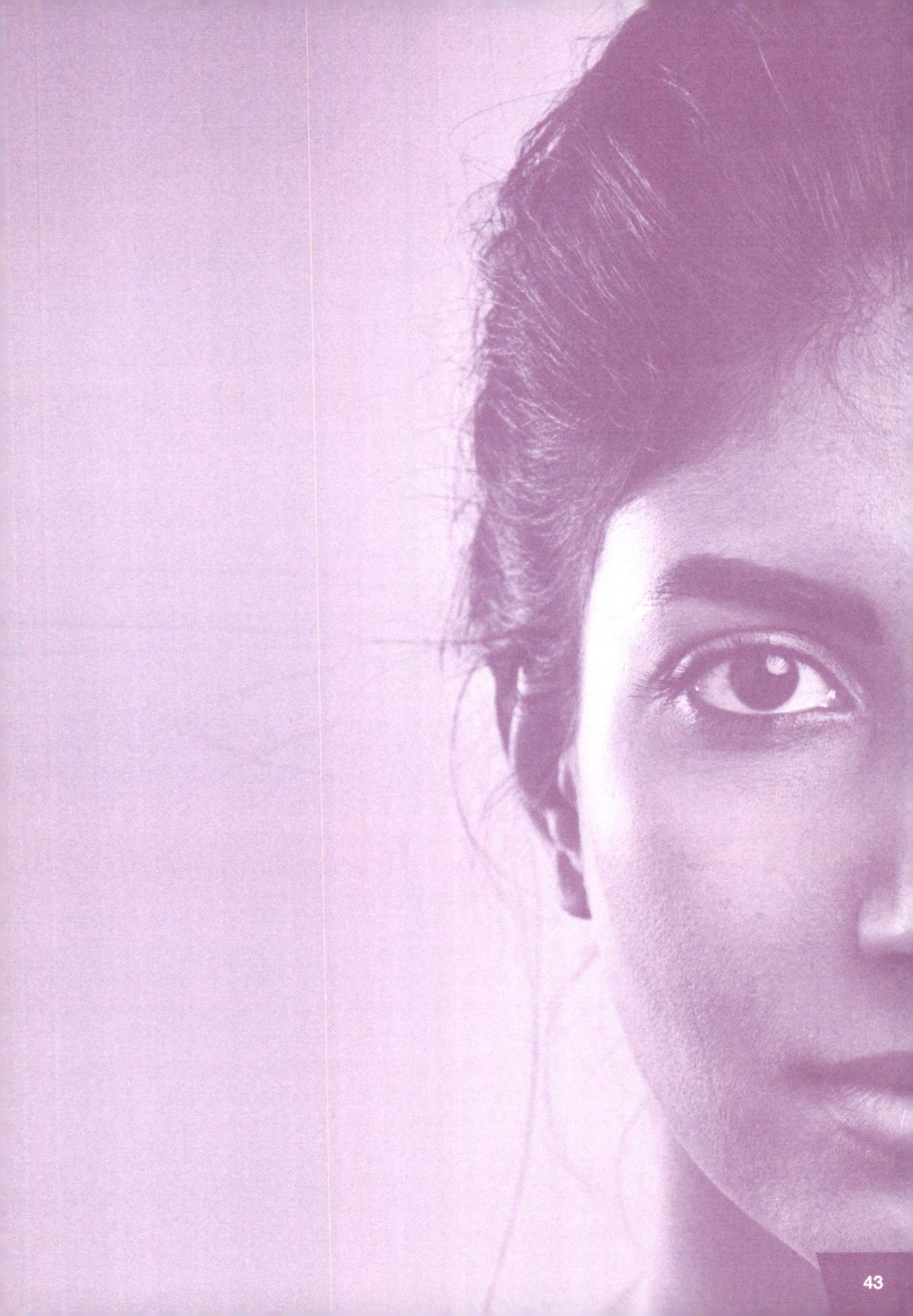

Respect itself say that this clear analysis of the less effective parts of programmes has pointed the way to further improving them.

The Mirabal researchers say that they began this work sceptical about whether men would choose to change, but now relate that: "After spending time with thousands of pages of transcripts of men and women talking about their use/experience of violence and abuse, we are convinced that our data shows steps towards change do start to happen for most". This is an unusually candid type of comment to add to an academic report and, coming from the leading feminist researchers in the whole field of domestic abuse, it is an extremely strong affirmation.

From these findings it is possible to have confidence that changing perpetrators of domestic abuse systematically can be attempted utilising these programmes, and by reaching out both to the police and the Criminal Justice System to further tackle abusers in the community.

This is timely because Article 16 of the Council of Europe Convention on preventing and combating violence against women requires signatories to "set up or support programmes aimed at teaching perpetrators of domestic violence to adopt non-violent behaviours" and the UK is likely to ratify this Convention shortly.

At this time there is also a cold economic challenge to tackle people who are expensive to police. Last year, 5,519 serial perpetrators accounted for 17,500 domestic abuse incidents in Northumbria - that is over half of all domestic incidents reported to the force. Many of the nine domestic homicides which occurred were committed by serial perpetrators and each is estimated to cost the public purse over £1m.

Fuelled by all these factors, the Office of the Police and Crime Commissioner for Northumbria set to work to shape a new process to identify and tackle serial perpetrators. We applied with partners, to the Police Innovation Fund for funding and are currently implementing the developed scheme, evaluating it as it progresses.

Central to our plans will be the creation of a Multi-Agency Tasking and Co-ordination process. This is a brand new mechanism that builds on an earlier model developed by the Scottish Police and so is to an extent experimental. It will complement existing processes for the management of high and medium risk victims of domestic abuse and for the management of violent and dangerous offenders. The first is done by a Multi-Agency Risk Assessment Conference where all the relevant public agencies come together to work out the safeguarding of a high-risk victim. Multi-Agency Public Protection Arrangements are the similarly constituted groups who jointly protect the public against dangerous offenders in the community. There will be links to Integrated Offender Management which is a method whereby police and the probation services supervise and scrutinise prolific and priority offenders. There will be a Multi-Agency Tasking and Co-ordination scheme in each of the three Area Commands in Northumbria Police, which each cover two local authorities.

The process will start when a serial perpetrator is identified using a Recency, Frequency and Gravity of offending method introduced by Police Scotland. They will be referred into Multi-Agency Tasking and Co-ordination process where the responsible agencies will work up a bespoke set of interventions, using a Domestic Abuse Toolkit. The toolkit is being developed and will provide partners with tactical options for targeting and disrupting the behaviour of perpetrators or for supporting perpetrators who want to address their behaviour. The relevant partners will meet periodically to review its effectiveness.

Three 26 week long serial perpetrator intervention courses will be added to our current local provision. They will have related victim programmes and will be delivered by a highly-rated local charity called Impact Family Services working with Barnardo's and with Gentoo, one of the region's largest social housing providers. Wearside Women in Need, who run domestic violence refuge and outreach services, will support the victims.

Gentoo has, almost uniquely, been prepared to remove perpetrators from family homes, in contrast to the traditional position that the women and children go away into a refuge. They have also been prepared to offer perpetrators alternative housing but only on agreement to strict conditions of residency such as signing an Acceptable Behaviour Agreement. The perpetrator scheme will make use of a similar condition; accommodation will be offered in return for completing a perpetrator programme. This is a key lever for use against perpetrators who are not facing charges but who may, for example, be the subject of safeguarding interventions. Gentoo will act in a consultancy capacity to other social housing providers so that they can establish and implement similar conditions.

The role of the Multi-Agency Tasking Co-ordinator is crucial. They will need to assess the most appropriate partners for engagement with the offender and avoid other partners being asked to attend unnecessary meetings, a significant complaint about Multi-Agency Risk Assessment Conferences. Together the partners, will decide which tactical options from the toolkit to use and the co-ordinator will take responsibility for ensuring that the overall strategy is developed and maintained and, for identifying the learning and best practice to share as the scheme unfolds.

This whole process for proactive identification of perpetrators and early intervention is quite separate from the Criminal Justice System. It can tackle serial perpetrators and offer safeguarding and support for victims who would not engage with the police and the courts, whether as a personal preference, because they are too tightly controlled by the perpetrator or for fear of reprisals. Northumbria Police will certainly prosecute wherever they can but the central point here is to identify serial perpetrators, through intelligent analysis of domestic violence calls to the police, via intelligence or through other agency reports.

There can then be intervention, through referral onto a perpetrator programme that we now know is likely to work or through whatever additional levers the Multi-Agency Tasking and Co-ordination partners can utilise, such as the housing provider putting conditions onto a tenancy or the police pursuing him for other offences. This way the perpetrator will understand that all the agencies will deal with him only on the basis that they expect him to change. This scheme shifts the focus from an obligation on the victim to engage with agencies in order to be safe and towards an obligation for the perpetrator to engage and to demonstrate what they are prepared to do to ensure that others are kept safe from the harm that they have inflicted.

The scheme is funded for two years and will be evaluated as it goes along, with an interim report and then a final one incorporating lessons learned in March 2017. The hope and expectation is that it will bring short and long term reduction in incidents of domestic abuse, cut domestic crime and, by reducing repeat offending by serial perpetrators, save a substantial amount of the estimated annual costs of domestic abuse in Northumbria of £559.4m so that those savings can be re-invested to sustain this model. A modest reduction of 20% in repeat Domestic Abuse would save over £250,000 of Police Officer time per annum, this alone would provide a two year pay back on the pilot funding.

The work of changing the behaviour of perpetrators, 87% of whose victims are women, is, clearly integral to ending domestic abuse. As a trustee of Respect I am pleased to be at the forefront of building on the rock of the Mirabal Project and on the former organisation's long-lived accreditation expertise with one of only six police forces which were not criticised by Her Majesty's Inspectorate of Constabulary for their handling of domestic abuse and who are determined to remain ahead of the game.

"It shows how far we have come with public policy making when we can say that we aim to make such a strategy an accepted component of workplace policy for a modern business, in the same way that risk strategies and equalities policies are now – to both of which domestic abuse is highly relevant."

04
WORKPLACES UNITE TO TACKLE DOMESTIC AND SEXUAL ABUSE

If you knock on the door of the Office of the Police and Crime Commissioner on a Friday morning, you might be surprised to find that actions speak louder than words.

You will find my staff working with other agencies training new Workplace Domestic and Sexual Abuse Champions so that they can provide much needed support to colleagues who are being abused at home by their partners.

In much the same way as employers now take on board health and safety training for staff, businesses, public authorities and voluntary and community sector employers in Northumbria, are appreciating the need for domestic and sexual abuse policies in the workplace. These say clearly to their workforce that they will support and help them if they are suffering from domestic or sexual abuse. Part of such a policy is agreement that selected employees can be trained as Workplace Domestic and Sexual Abuse Champions. Those employees learn how to see the signs of possible abuse and how to deal with any disclosure calmly, passing the colleague on to a domestic abuse outreach worker or another source of advice and support.

Our overall quest to tackle domestic and sexual abuse from as many angles as possible, led us to appreciate that the public were concerned but not well-informed about it. If we could explain how disabling abuse can be, we felt confident that many ordinary people would be prepared to help friends or acquaintances who were in its grip. The question was which sections of the public should we start with on our mission to inform and engage?

Domestic and sexual abuse can extract a cost not only from the individual and their family but also from their employer and co-employees because people who are being undermined by abuse will not be working optimally. That appreciation led us to think that employers and people in the workplace would be a good place to start. We would engage the working public first.

Domestic abuse is not about a black eye or an occasional drunken row, it is a deliberate course of conduct to control the partner. Violence is certainly used, together with the threat of it as well as sexual abuse, but the perpetrator will also undermine the confidence and the autonomy of the partner. Friends and family will not be welcome at the home. She - for 87% of victims are female - will be starved of money; told she's worthless; told she's ugly and stupid; that the children don't like her and she is lucky to have the perpetrator because nobody else would want her. By the time she realises that this is abuse she will have been separated from all her sources of support and will see herself as so unworthy that she is not likely to be believed if she complains. She will be trapped.

Abuse will often impact on how she performs her job. In 2009, domestic abuse cost businesses in productivity and output almost £2bn through physical injury alone and the costs of related psychological damage are likely to be greater still. Symptoms of domestic abuse can include depression, anxiety, distraction or problems with concentration. This will show in changes to the quality of the victim's work; often for no apparent reason. There may be lateness, reflecting his behaviour in the morning when she should be leaving for work, and absenteeism when she is hurt, bruised or so demoralised that she cannot face seeing her work colleagues. There may be frequent time off for medical appointments; inappropriate or excessive clothing (to hide injuries or because of being locked out of home and wardrobe) and an increased turnover of staff who are sometimes even coerced into giving up their job, precisely to cut off the avenue of escape that we want every workplace to offer.

A recent Domestic Homicide Review in Northumbria showed

that 'J' the subject of the review was known to police, had attended A&E, was subject to Safeguarding, had attended marriage guidance, retained a solicitor and had been to her GP several times with suspected injuries. Each of these agencies knew a part of the story but the person who knew more than all of them was her line manager, in whom she confided at work. Through no fault of his own, the manager did not know what to do with the information he had, beyond offering a shoulder to cry on. A workplace policy could have guided him and perhaps made a difference.

There is a contrasting account from Ms 'F' now a senior banker, who tells her story at our business recruitment conferences. She was suffering from extreme and persistent domestic and sexual abuse from her partner, so much that she was hospitalised. Her manager had to visit her to recover a set of workplace keys. She told him how she received her injuries and the employer determined to help. He gave her paid time away from work to make arrangements and then one day she set out for the bank, as usual, but she didn't go to the branch round the corner but to one three hundred miles away to which her employer had arranged a transfer. Management carefully planned the move with 'F' without telling her colleagues where she had gone. When her partner came looking for her, not only was she no longer there but her colleagues were able to say that they did not know where she was. 'F' tells our conferences that, in her view, her employer saved her life.

There is also the shocking and tragic story of Jane Clough. She had moved in with her parents at an address unknown to her partner after she'd reported him for repeatedly raping her. Unbelievably, he was bailed by the court. Although there was a condition on bail that he should not approach her, he had been sexually abusing and controlling her for some time and was not going to let her go. Still less did he intend her to be able to give evidence which might put him in prison. He found her at the hospital which was her workplace and stabbed her to death in the car park. It is a great tribute to her that her parents, John and Penny, now frequently travel from the North West to address our recruiting conferences and to convince employers that they have a role to play in stopping others from suffering similarly.

Victims may be at increased risk of harm in their workplace if they leave an abusive partner, as it may be the only place where they can be found.

In contrast, prior to separation, the workplace may be the one place the victim goes without the violent and controlling partner; a safe haven from what is happening at home.

In an attempt to make it easy for employers to respond, we have designed our own template employers' policy which sets out clear procedures and pathways and is easily adaptable for most kinds of workplace. We feature this policy at our free introductory conferences of which there have already been more than a dozen, focussing on specific kinds of business, on one occasion solicitors and on another local housing providers. We are also providing free training so that if a business joins up they can select management and employees who are suitable to become Domestic and Sexual Violence Champions; people who can be trained to be a confidential, sympathetic and well-informed first point of contact. Further training is also available and includes information about culturally specific forms of abuse such as forced marriage, so-called honour based violence and Female Genital Mutilation whilst making clear that straightforward domestic and sexual abuse crosses cultural barriers and can be even harder for a member of a minority group to report. Newcastle City Council has been with us since the beginning of this quest and has taken the extra step of engaging the charity Respect to monitor and evaluate the impact of their own policy. They will share the results with us and we will learn lessons from them.

We are working with the North East Chamber of Commerce, the Institute of Directors, small and medium enterprises as well as public authorities and the voluntary and community sector to promote this endeavour. Some employers already have good policies but welcome the addition of a team of champions to make sure it is a living policy. Local trade unions such as Unison and GMB have given us great support and are an obvious source of good DSVA champions.

The Champions need a system of mutual support and we have developed Champions Networks and a series of confidential online groups. These will support and develop the training and facilitate confidential interaction amongst the champions to help each other. It is also a source of personal support should an individual Champion themselves need counselling or advice perhaps having been the recipient of harrowing information from a victim.

There are six Networks so far, supported by a steering group including the six local authority domestic violence leads and other relevant partners from the statutory and voluntary sectors.

We have over 350 public and voluntary sector champions and a significant additional number scattered differentially across the 30 varied businesses that have now joined up, about 130 in total. The businesses range from Intu who run the physical and managerial infrastructure for Eldon Square which is the biggest shopping centre in Europe, to Dicksons, Family Pork Butchers based in South Shields. We have some Champions in schools, in our libraries and swimming pools, local Soroptimists may feel able to play this role and we are ambitious to get more champions into members clubs and organisations of all kinds.

In the North East alone during 2012-13 there were 53,491 incidents of domestic violence reported to police, the vast majority with female victims. However the Crime Survey of England and Wales suggests that less than 30 per cent of domestic abuse incidents ever get reported and we are trying to play a role in changing that. We want to offer a confidential non-criminal justice based lifeline for some of the women who would not otherwise report. We can do that by placing good, well-trained people in places where it may be possible for a victim to speak out.

It shows how far we have come with public policy making when we can say that we aim to make such a strategy an accepted component of workplace policy for a modern business, in the same way that risk strategies and equalities policies are now – to both of which domestic abuse is highly relevant. Our work found its way into the Labour Women's Safety Commission Report in 2014 and the Welsh Government came close to making it compulsory by law to have a Workplace Domestic and Sexual Abuse Policy. Now, our DVSA Policy and Champions have been included in the North East Better Health at Work Award Criteria for 2015 which is a matter of great pride and has given recruitment both of employers and champions a significant boost.

"The scheme is creating opportunities for victims, learning for police and agencies and a strong ethic of active day to day partnership working that is unusually close and mutually supportive."

05
DVSA CARS: A NEW SERVICE FOR DOMESTIC VIOLENCE VICTIMS

Written by Vera Baird QC and Clare Phillipson, Director of Wearside Women in Need

Why did 28,000 domestic abuse calls to Northumbria Police a year lead to only 2,000 – 3,000 criminal convictions? Do thousands of victims therefore, continue to face abuse despite their calls for help?

Her Majesty's Inspectorate of Constabulary see Northumbria as a force which responds well to domestic abuse and we work constantly to improve but victims themselves often do not want a prosecution. Though forced to call police in fear of attack, in the longer term many callers are more afraid of the process and consequences of prosecuting this very personal crime against their partner. He may control them too strongly for court even to be a possibility or perhaps affection or a sense of responsibility, remarkably, is still in play. The suspicion is that, indeed, many callers, despite their obvious cry for help are – perhaps the right term is - helplessly - continuing to suffer from domestic abuse. This cannot continue. How could we add value to those police callouts?

The commitment became that the police would connect local victims with local support, irrespective of whether a crime had been committed or a prosecution was sought. We would piggy-back expert help from our friends in the refuge movement onto police 999 calls to offer practical and emotional support.

We developed a pilot scheme called 'the DVSA cars'. It is a ground breaking way to respond and it was speedily adopted force-wide. The initials stand for Domestic Violence Support and Assistance and the service ensures that a specially trained officer and a domestic abuse worker go together to relevant 999 calls. Literally, the closest possible police response vehicle will attend to resolve the emergency but in a domestic abuse case the DVSA car is also despatched.

When there is a call, officers will arrest or remove the perpetrator in some way and with the complainant's consent, the DVSA worker will come in. She is a trained professional; many of the women on our rota for this role have worked in the domestic abuse world for years. They are well able to gain the confidence of the victim and to hear their story. We are told that many victims are not clear that they are, in fact, suffering abuse; that many do understand but have no-one to turn to; some simply do not know what else they can do. The worker will offer whatever it takes so that the victim is no longer alone. Occasionally people have asked to be taken away and housed in a refuge there and then; many want to meet later, in secret, to consider their options. The DVSA worker will seek to capture the history as well as the events of that night to better assess the level of risk and advise appropriately. They can tell victims what services the police can supply, what powers they and the police can use and what services, beyond the police, are available to support them. They will make clear that the victim is not necessarily expected to make decisions at all at this stage or indeed, ever, but that the DVSA worker will be available for her, in effect at any time and any place. The lack of law enforcement status and power mean sometimes that a victim will disclose more to a domestic abuse worker than they would to a police officer. There is less fear of consequences and a better sense that the worker is dedicated to her and not to police statistics or to the court process.

The specialist officer may play a key role or not depending on what arises. Specialist cars and body worn cameras are supporting this service and there will be a video record from the moment the team arrived. Police have power, on their own initiative, to make a Domestic Violence Protection Notice against a perpetrator, ordering him from the premises for 48 hours with a possible extension, from magistrates, to 28 days. But the victim may want no formal action to be taken at all.

The scheme means that the available support is comprehensive and holistic. In the past the crisis situation was driven by 'immediacy'. Now although the police officer at the scene is clearly able to utilise legal measures and deal with the perpetrator, the specialist support worker will listen to the victim, and focus on the situation from a victim outcome perspective.

The presence of the DVSA worker helps trust to be established and rapport to be built up so that even if what happens is a series of further calls, police will continue to be responsive but with a better understanding of the victim's situation. This lends itself to implementing longer term preventative packages. The follow up work done in the days after the incident by the domestic violence support worker with or without police involvement, enables victims to appreciate that they do have support and can take practical steps to escape their situation, with or without prosecuting or getting injunctions. This dual approach of crisis intervention with long term support and crime prevention benefits both the victim and the wider policing agenda. Clearly each individual victim has different needs, and may have total clarity about what they want or don't want to happen. But victims can be fearful and cautious of taking action, while the police are 'fearful' of being seen to not take action.

The team will consider jointly all aspects of safeguarding, including the completion of the Domestic Abuse, Stalking and Honour Based Violence risk assessment form. The multi-disciplinary skills create a dynamic approach to the process and ensure that risk assessments are comprehensive and very detailed. It is a credit to those working with us on this scheme in Northumbria that they take the opportunity to learn from each other.

There is a DVSA car with a joint team in place on the peak demand nights of Friday, Saturday and Sunday in Northumbria's two highest demand areas, the cities of Newcastle and Sunderland.

The scheme has evolved and offers additional interventions in quiet times too, when the DVSA cars are more akin to women's safety patrols. Officers are focused on women, children and violence, and with expertise on board, the patrols stop to check on women and take action to protect those who look vulnerable on the streets. Although difficult to quantify this is likely to be very effective in terms of crime prevention. Ensuring that distressed women, young women, and women

Photograph of Clare Phillipson, Director of Wearside Women in Need
Courtesy of the Sunderland Echo

who appear to be drunk stay safe, have support, and perhaps are taken home could prove invaluable in driving down street crimes against women. About 40 individuals who appeared to be at risk have been helped, either taken to hospital, taken home, taken to a refuge or engaged with social services and a number of children under the age of 10 have been found out on the streets after midnight and kept safe.

During quiet periods too, police officers use the time to discuss domestic violence and abuse and to learn more of the victim perspective from specialist staff. In effect having a one to one training session is a great opportunity. It will add to officers' confidence to respond more effectively to victims. Specialist domestic abuse staff, in turn, take the chance to learn more about the difficulties and frustrations police officers face in attempting to prosecute cases, and the legal limitations in some situations which they might help to overcome.

In addition to the domestic abuse workers out on patrol, full time DVSA staff are located in police stations. They ensure that the night's work is followed up and co-ordinated effectively. These DVSA workers work closely with the patrol workers and their organisations as well as with neighbourhood beat teams who manage lower risk victims, to ensure all-round support. This has further boosted the service offered to victims and sustained the multi-disciplinary approach. The full time workers deliver awareness training to front line staff and feed back to both disciplines to make improvements in operating the scheme.

Wearside Women in Need and the HOPE Consortium, the two specialist organisations who supply the DVSA patrol workers, report that for victims, the scheme has been a resounding success.

It has engaged with 155 DV victims, 153 female and 2 males with only 12 callers refusing the service. A remarkable 92% of people contacted in this way, accepted help, support and ongoing engagement after the initial call out. Only 30 of those people had been involved with services before which means that in the vast majority of cases, the scheme was giving support to people who had never engaged with any professional help. Prior to the DVSA scheme I had asked police officers to hand out the Wearside Women in Need helpline number when attending call outs but there was only a 1% take up from victims, making 92% a dramatic improvement.

We extended the cover at peak times for example during the World Cup and over Christmas and provided continuous cover from the 19th December 2014 till the 3rd Jan 2015 including covering some days such as New Year's Eve, from 4pm - 4am.

In March the DVSA car attended a call from a male wanting his girlfriend removed from the property as she was causing trouble. Clare the DVSA worker tells the story:

"On arrival we spoke to the response officers who were already there. The woman 'suspect' had cried and said that she had nowhere to go but was worried for her safety where she was. The officers brought her outside and we approached her to see if she was OK, from our intelligence, she has been the victim of DV within this relationship for some time. My concern was that she was in a serious situation with much more to the incident than she was saying to the police. I explained who I was and what our service was and she disclosed an incident the day before where she was strangled by her partner and said she had been assaulted that afternoon. This progressed into a situation where the partner was arrested, the victim taken from the property to refuge accommodation and referred for specialist support. If the DVSA car had not attended, the victim would not have disclosed anything regarding her situation or any of the previous attacks".

In the spring of 2015, in Newcastle Jessica another DVSA worker was on patrol when a male called the police saying his girlfriend had threatened to jump off Byker Bridge after an argument. This is Jessica's note:

"The DVSA driver spotted the girlfriend walking towards the bridge and stopped. I talked to her and she disclosed that her relationship was very controlling and she had been suffering DV. We told her about the services that were available to help and that she was not alone in this. She said that she had no friends and did not want to be with her parents, so we told her about the refuge and safe places she could go. We completed the DASH form. It showed that she had previously had her head banged off a wall. She was eventually taken to a safe address and she told me that she wanted someone to talk to about her relationship as she was depressed and upset. West End Women and Girls Centre was discussed and she wanted someone to contact her".

This incident initially came in as a 'Vulnerable Woman' but through the work and time that the DVSA car can give to victims it transpired she was in an abusive relationship and that she was so depressed she wanted to kill herself and had threatened this before. Now, she can access the support she requires.

We have always hoped that refuge outreach staff working openly with officers would demonstrate to complainants that it is safe to put trust in the police. A hoped-for result is that more victims will agree to take their perpetrator to court. This cannot be more than a footnote to the support for a victim, which is the principal point of the scheme, but prosecutions are important. Perpetrators commit crimes and are often serial offenders, moving, if a first victim escapes, to another and another.

DVSA worker, Clare, suggests that this is beginning to occur:

"One officer was speaking with a victim of a domestic violence assault who was reluctant to provide a statement and attend court. After speaking with our DVSA car she was fully on board and provided a statement. This is a clear demonstration of the trust that can be built with a victim and the evidential benefits of it".

The learning goes on. Officers themselves have recently suggested that when they are working the DVSA car they should be in plain clothes. This would be less daunting for victims and might add to their willingness to talk. Some officers have noticed that victims 'clam up' as soon as they see the uniform, so we will pilot a plain clothes DVSA car to see if it can make a difference.

What started as a paper exercise to find some way of improving outcomes for victims uninterested in the Criminal Justice System has become a living reality. Not only do victims appreciate it but the agencies we work with and officers themselves are taking it to heart. It is surprising that the traditionally territorial police were prepared to let women refuge workers join them, literally on the frontline, though it is less striking that the DVSA workers have taken the opportunity to tell the police, as the gatekeepers to the Criminal Justice System, what victims really want. The scheme is creating opportunities for victims, learning for police and agencies and a strong ethic of active day to day partnership working that is unusually close and mutually supportive. We believe this scheme should be taken up elsewhere, with the potential to help transform the policing of domestic abuse nationwide.

06 PUTTING VICTIMS FIRST

07 CHANGING POLICE CULTURE BY POSITIVELY HANDLING COMPLAINTS

08 SEEING IS BELIEVING: NORTHUMBRIA'S COURT OBSERVERS

09 THE FIRST TRIAL: COURT OBSERVERS TELL THE STORY

10 PROJECT SANCTUARY: TARGETING SEXUAL EXPLOITATION AND WORKING WITH OTHERS TO PROTECT THE VULNERABLE

11 PROGRESS AGAINST DOMESTIC ABUSE THROUGH UNDERSTANDING COERCIVE CONTROL

12 WE NEED OUR HUMAN RIGHTS – DISPELLING THE MYTHS

13 FIGHTING FOR FAIR FUNDING FROM GOVERNMENT

SECTION 2

IMPROVING THE CRIMINAL JUSTICE SYSTEM

"The police referrals are generated by a needs assessment, undertaken by the officer at the point of reporting a crime. This is a unique point of the Northumbria model; not all police forces visit every victim of crime – we do. This gives our police the opportunity to talk direct to a victim and try to best understand and assess their cope and recovery needs."

06
PUTTING VICTIMS FIRST

> Victims of crime are not given the prominence they deserve by the criminal justice agencies. Until recently, they have been almost an afterthought, but this archaic approach is on the cusp of change.

Going to court as a victim can be a traumatic experience. It may worsen the personal impact of the crime. Victims First Northumbria supports victims from the earliest stage to give the best chance of coping and recovery, whatever has happened, with a court case or not.

My office in Northumbria fields a team of volunteer Court Observers who watch the trial process in Newcastle Crown Court with an eye, in particular, on how victims of rape are treated. We see from the work of the Observers and the experience of Victims First Northumbria as more of its clients go to court, that we will gain good information about how the system treats victims. We will develop a victim advocacy campaign, to analyse any concerns and argue for change.

The current Government's journey to improve victim services began in January 2012 with the consultation document 'Getting it Right for Victims and Witnesses'. They subsequently decided to delegate some victim services to Police and Crime Commissioners so that they would fit local needs more accurately. Our responsibility was to start in April of this year, so there was a lot to do.

To help smooth the way, in May 2013 the Ministry of Justice published a commissioning framework for victim services.

A driving force is Baroness Newlove, the Government's Victims' Commissioner, whose vision is that every victim has a Victim Care Manager who will work one to one supporting them on their cope and recovery journey. This resonated well as my vision for Northumbria started to emerge.

There are changes countrywide and other Police and Crime Commissioners are taking a very mixed approach. Avon and Somerset have totally revamped their victim services, bringing the core service in house with support from partners and local agencies.

Cambridgeshire has introduced a police-led victim hub with support being delivered via their own volunteer network. Others are entering into short term contracts with providers while they continue to work out exactly what it is they want to deliver for the victims in their area. Some are staying with the status quo.

The Government still commissions some work nationally. This includes an information line for victims, the homicide service; rape support centres; help for victims of trafficking and the court based witness service. Having a national contract for the witness service, which is present in every court, presumably makes commercial sense and the specialist homicide service has insufficient demand to justify local provision. However, it is unhelpful to have a mixture of commissioning in areas like rape support. It is curious too that Police and Crime Commissioners themselves, although they have a statutory obligation to support victims are only funded until the end of this financial year. There is an urgent need to rationalise the whole of victim funding.

We tested demand by consulting on what victims want, what services are available and where the gaps are. We are now sure that we understand our landscape and our partners.

We have a particular focus on vulnerable or repeat victims and those with the greatest need, although our aim is to deliver good service to everyone. There is no bar on anyone who needs help, such as parents, siblings, children, partners and close friends since we recognise that trauma can adversely affect those who are close to a victim.

The Northumbria vision for victim services states: "Our vision is to create a Northumbria area where victims of crime feel confident to seek help and when they do, they are provided with a choice of high quality support tailored to meet their individual needs".

A unique point about our model is that where the police are called they will do the needs assessment using a pro forma developed by Victims First Northumbria. Not all police forces attend every criminal offence but Northumbria does, albeit, sometimes in less urgent cases by appointment a few hours later. The officer will agree a safety plan and an investigation plan, so a little extra questioning is needed to ascertain support needs. Victims attach to the investigating officer and find this reassuring. Officers say they are better motivated by understanding the impact of crimes and we think the victim is better for feeling central to the justice process from the start. We did not set out to replace existing specialist in-force services such as Family Liaison Officers who already place the victim at the heart of an investigation.

If a victim wants support, their details are passed straight to Victims First Northumbria who will make contact, within 48 hours. There is no need to repeat what happened. The Victim Care Co-ordinator will rely on the officer's work so that we can minimise the number of times the victim has to relive their experience. However, we make clear that Victims First Northumbria is a service independent of the police and we make a separate relationship with the victim. Occasionally an officer will detect that a victim does not want to discuss their needs with the police and will pass the assessment job directly to Victims First Northumbria.

Police and Crime Commissioners are allocated a budget from the Ministry of Justice in order to commission support services for victims of crime to help them 'cope' in the short term with the immediate impact of their crime and to 'recover' from more serious impacts where appropriate. This has allowed local patterns and volume of crime to be put together with local knowledge of the specialist organisations who can provide that support. Previously, commissioning was undertaken nationally by the Ministry of Justice for many of these services and other locally based services were left to fund raise for themselves.

Duplication that existed in the previous arrangements has been significantly streamlined. For example victims would receive an initial needs assessment from a police officer, then would be needs assessed again when passed to the former victims' agency. If that victim had been subjected to a serious sexual crime they may have been allocated a Sexual Offences Liaison Officer, if referred for a forensic examination would also be allocated an Independent Sexual Violence Adviser, a further support person. In the event that a court case followed the joint Crown Prosecution Service/ Police Witness Care Unit would again assess their needs. Within a short time after the crime a victim could have several needs assessment and a number of supporters. Now there is only one primary supporter and one shared needs assessment.

The Victim Care Co-ordinators undertake most immediate care and support needs. Previously, volunteers did a significant proportion of this work but now the new arrangements provide much better co-ordination of support services from employed staff.

Victims First Northumbria now work with victims according to need – not according to crime type which was formally the case. For example, an older person who has had a garden shed broken into and who is terrified of her home being invaded will receive support from Victims First Northumbria, despite this being an apparently 'minor' crime which would not until now have entitled her to any support.

Importantly, people who do not report to the police can get support. We offer contact by phone, online or text and have a promotional campaign in libraries and other community contact points. People self-refer and third parties ask for help for colleagues and friends. Sometimes social services ask for help for an existing client who has become a victim and Victims First Northumbria will discuss which agency should take the lead. Around 10% of Victims First Northumbria's clients have not reported the crime to the police. Their needs, as victims, are just as significant as those of the people who do.

Whether done by police or by our own Victim Care Co-ordinators, the assessment will help Victims First Northumbria to discuss initial emotional and practical support and/or refer on for specialist help. We also have a network of volunteers who will befriend a victim taking them through a programme towards recovery. The Supporting Victims Fund, which is the balance of Ministry of Justice funding after the costs of Victims First Northumbria has enabled us to enhance and strengthen the overall offer to victims in Northumbria. We have commissioned expertise to cover gaps in services for domestic and sexual abuse, young people under 18, supporting victims of

69

hate crime and victims with mental health needs.

We recruited care co-ordinators with diversity in mind, to provide a culturally sympathetic response for most victims. We wanted men and women, young and old, gay, lesbian and transsexual, Black and Minority Ethnic and people of all abilities. Additionally, each co-ordinator has taken on a specialism such as dementia support or working with those with learning disabilities. This effort has made me very proud of the people there who do a huge amount, on their own initiative, of what would usually be termed: 'Going the extra mile'.

Victims First Northumbria will stay available even if a case is referred on. We interpret Baroness Newlove's vision of a single co-ordinator as requiring us to be there, should a referral fail, prove to be unsuitable or for any other reason, until the victim themselves chooses to step down from further support. It is also arguable that the Victims First Northumbria co-ordinator should be involved in the notification of court dates and preparation for hearings. The court liaison function is currently carried out by police and goes wider than victims, including notice of court dates to officers and non-victim witnesses. However, receiving a court date is associated in many cases, with a victim's decision to drop out. Integrating the liaison function in cases where victims have a Victims First Northumbria care package would combine another opportunity for streamlining contact with a key chance to give extra support at that especially stressful time.

A snapshot in September 2015 shows Victims First Northumbria receiving 3,977 referrals since April (double the number getting support before Victims First Northumbria). 3,377 cases have been completed successfully whilst 0.4% of cases were outside the remit of the organisation. The team currently have 600 active cases; 52% of referrals are repeat victims, in some cases people already working with Victims First Northumbria, 38% are vulnerable, and 30% of cases are referred on to organisations such as LGBT support, rape and domestic abuse services, specialist young peoples' organisations, talking therapies, housing organisations and Citizens Advice.

Victims have experienced a wide range of offences. Almost 20% have suffered an assault with injury and a further 10% a common assault, almost 40% of these assaults are domestic abuse offences, 10% of cases are damage to a dwelling, 9% are house burglaries and 11% are damage to motor vehicles.

In court, the rights of the defendant have, correctly, always been uppermost but both victims and defendants are vulnerable in the Criminal Justice System. Through the long-established presumption of innocence defendants are treated respectfully by the courts. What does our unwritten constitution tell us about how to treat victims?

They are not parties to the case. It isn't a trial between the complainant and the defendant like a civil action when A sues B for damages for injury in a car accident. A prosecution is brought by the Crown on behalf of the public and the victim is merely there as a witness. S/he is nobody's client; nobody represents him/her. There is a public duty on witnesses to give evidence to support the proper prosecution of offences. Nobody knows if they are telling the truth, mistaken or lying, so they are summoned to court and handed over to the parties. They are commodities for the trial and beyond ordinary courtesy from the judge, they have few rights. They are used by the parties to make their points.

In recent times, victims have received care, in the sense in which Victims First Northumbria can give it, by reassuring that they are not to blame, telling them that the state cares that they have been wronged and helping to rebuild broken morale, analogous to hospital care for a patient. This has been contested on the basis that it may strengthen the victim's ability to testify or, somehow prime them unfairly against the defendant. Court-based victim care has been harder to achieve. Defendants have to show that the same 'victims' are wrong, lying, vindictive. If the state shows them respect in the face of a jury, it may imply that it believes them, undermining the presumption of innocence.

However, the shock impact of crime and nervousness around court attendance are now better understood. Victims are catered for with a familiarisation visit to an empty court before the trial. They are often entitled to testify over a TV link or from behind a screen. These 'special measures' are commonplace. They separate the victim from the defendant, take away the spotlight of being in court and feel kind, but they don't protect them from their status as a commodity in the adversarial system.

Victims can be built up after a crime through victim care only to be broken down again by cross examination. Victims of child sexual abuse, rape and hate crime say that they are questioned roughly by use of myths and prejudices to save the person who raped them yet nobody

Are you a victim of crime?

VICTIMS FIRST gives support and advice to victims of crime throughout Northumbria.

0800 011 3116
www.victimsfirstnorthumbria.org.uk
Monday to Friday 8am – 8pm and Saturday 9am – 5pm

Victimsfirst

in authority is concerned because this is how we do trials. They come away re-scarred, and alienated from the justice system which they will never help again. Yet it is the unarguable right of the defendant to protect himself from wrongful conviction by attacking the evidence.

This unresolved dilemma has brought victim care to the heart of the trial process where it should always have been. Courts must learn not to turn back the recovery clock whilst ensuring a proper defence.

Prosecution lawyers are now expected to reassure the witness that someone is on their side by meeting them, for a chat, before the case. Recent high profile rape and sexual abuse trials have educated courts and the public as to the extreme sensitivity of some victims. Long investigations and resource-intensive Rotherham-like trials must sustain vulnerable witnesses or face collapse. Applications to cross examine a rape complainant about previous sexual history require judges to allow or reject them question by question, multi-defendant trials where small children have been questioned by up to ten barristers have led to strict rules against repetition and overlap. Precedents are growing which control the extent of questioning and discourage overbearing flamboyance or personal attack.

For the future, the Director of Public Prosecutions wants victims to be told the defence and likely areas of questioning, not just thrust into court with no knowledge of the issues. I want judges to bust rape myths for the jury at the start of trials and not, as now, at the end.

Police are trained to give evidence, the defendant plans his case with his lawyers. In 21st century Britain we leave only victim/witnesses vulnerably high and dry.

But Police and Crime Commissioners are responsible for victims and have a statutory duty, to promote and support an efficient and effective Criminal Justice System. These two roles have not been united before and they offer a renewed prospect for a balanced understanding of the two. In Northumbria we hope to learn by that dual engagement and advocate for fair change.

"A key objective is to learn lessons from this work and make changes as we move forward. We need to understand why people complain, improve our services to match and make a difference. Analysis of complaints will improve our understanding of what concerns local people."

07
CHANGING POLICE CULTURE BY POSITIVELY HANDLING COMPLAINTS

> All too often, allegations of minor police misconduct can reflect badly on a force. Unless the complaints system handles them appropriately, concern or annoyance from the original behaviour will be followed by total alienation and damaging loss of confidence.

How serious complaints are handled is set out by legislation, but at lower level complaints should be resolved quickly and efficiently. In July 2014, the Independent Police Complaints Commission and Ipsos MORI survey found that whilst the public felt they were able to complain, they were often confused about the best way to voice their dissatisfaction. 33% of those surveyed were not confident their complaint would be handled fairly.

The truth is in this country we have a very complex police complaints system which is overly bureaucratic, over-legalistic and overly focused on blame – this still applies nationally, but here in Northumbria we have worked hard to try to bring change in areas of police-public relations that the legislation does not circumscribe.

Change had to happen. Northumbria Police is a high performing force. It has an exceptional 92% satisfaction for tackling anti-social behaviour and is always in the top few forces nationwide whatever is being counted. However, one of the first reports to land on my desk as the newly elected Police and Crime Commissioner came from the House of Commons Home Affairs Select Committee. It showed that between April 2011 and March 2012, Northumbria Police were successfully appealed in respect complaints than any other force. The Independent Police Complaints Commission upheld 53% of 146 appeals, the national average was 38% with some forces having a score of only 15%.

The report documented the wider context of the public's well-known distrust of "police investigating police" and the notorious cases such as Hillsborough and Orgreave, which have shown police to be defensive or even downright dishonest in connection with complaints against them.

Turning back to Northumbria, I decided to post myself in the Professional Standards Department in order to read each and every one of the successful appeals.

Some examples demonstrate what I found:

A woman came home to find police in her kitchen and her front door off its hinges. They were looking for her son who didn't live there. Nobody had asked her where he was. They got up to leave and she asked about the door. They would call someone who charged £40 to block it up temporarily. But she needed a working front door. They left. She couldn't repair it until pay day so the house was insecure and her home insurance invalidated until then. This is ridiculous; police should be protecting community safety not endangering it. The 'defence' that police had a magistrates' warrant was continued by their Professional Standards Department until the Independent Police Complaints Commission shot it down. The situation looked simple to me. The intelligence used to get the warrant was wrong so why not apologise, pay up and mend the door?

In another case a young woman, supported by the evidence of a male passer-by and a doctor's note, claimed that she had a very minor head injury from being pushed by police at a demonstration. She hadn't got the officer's number and nobody admitted it, so the police wrote to her to tell her that it couldn't have happened. No wonder she appealed. To a push add an accusation of lying inferentially against the stranger witness too.

Why not explain that without a complaint there was no outcome. They had tried their best and apologised for however her injury had occurred and wished her well.

Overall, the responses were characterised by defensiveness, antagonism to those who complained and a sense that the police could never admit being wrong. What was puzzling was that complaints were not all dealt with in Northumbria's Professional Standards Department, most are still handled by inspectors in the area commands. These are officers who, in this basically very good force, would put themselves out to tackle a complaint of crime or anti-social behaviour and go the extra mile for any member of the public. Why was the attitude to complaints so different?

I gave a detailed report of my findings to the Chief Constable who changed the personnel in Professional Standards Department and passed my report on to the officer in charge, but I decided to make more than that change.

My first instruction was to make the process simple. I removed the need for a member of the public to have to visit a police station and wait until an Inspector was free to take a complaint. Now complaints come to one central point, my office, and can be delivered by letter, email, website and telephone. I've even followed up complaints raised on Twitter.

I identified four key objectives:

- To ensure complaints were dealt with quickly and efficiently
- The process is simple for staff and complainants, and residents do not have to follow a complex procedure to lodge a complaint
- There is an outcome and lessons are learnt
- Complainants change their view of Northumbria Police and confidence is restored

From January 2014, we have had a 'Triage Team' in my office. Three Complaints Service Advisors are seconded from police civilian staff to be the first point of contact for complaints. These Complaints Service Advisors have no background of working in Professional Standards Department, but have been selected for their commitment to customer service. They are new to this specific role, though experienced people, and do not bring with them any of the old culture or habits from Professional Standards Department. On the other hand, they are trusted by the police, as reliable employees who understand that police sometimes do have to deal firmly with the public. We regard this as an important component if we are to keep the confidence and hence the co-operation of police, through what is clearly an innovative and potentially challenging new process.

If we could separate complaints from the discipline system we could do even better. Officers are not likely to help resolve even minor complaints if their disciplinary file will be noted. Our branch of the Police Federation discussed the proposals with us and joined in. We agreed that any response from an officer to a triage level complaint could not be used, if the triage failed. In any subsequent disciplinary proceedings, Professional Standards Department must start again. The Office of the Police and Crime Commissioner's Business Manager and a Police Inspector visited every Area Command and every Department to describe the purpose, aims and nature of the work that the Triage Team are carrying out, making sure that their role is clearly understood.

Finally, the Complaints Service Advisors carry the authority of both the Chief Constable and the Police and Crime Commissioner and there have been few in the force who have resisted helping this process along.

The Complaints Service Advisors are proactive. On receipt of a complaint they ring the sender, definitely within 24 hours (many cases show them ringing within two hours) and listen. They try to resolve the problem over the phone or can arrange a home visit. They will offer an explanation or speak to the officer and their supervisor, who will provide their perspective. If they have got it wrong, they can say so. The atmosphere is gradually changing so that instead of getting a black mark for a minor complaint, officers are praised for entering into its resolution.

I make the point whenever I talk to our officers, that we need community support and every person alienated is one fewer supporter, so we must try to regain their friendship.

Compare this speedy, friendly, well-informed contact with the traditional practice of a 'holding letter' received seven days (at least) after the submission of a complaint. Now, about 60% of our complaints are not in play after 7 days. We are signalling to the complainant that:

- We care about what they are telling us
- We want to understand fully what their concerns are
- Most importantly we want to help and find a resolution as fast as possible

There have been many successes:

A simple case was where a resident who had tried to get his laptop back from Northumbria Police, grew exasperated at delay and complained. Within an hour of a Complaints Service Advisor receiving the complaint, he had picked up his laptop.

A resident was unhappy with where the police had located a CCTV camera and felt oppressed by it, Triage got partners together to find an alternative location.

The law requires police complaints to be recorded within ten days of receipt. This gives the Complaints Service Advisor a window of opportunity to try and resolve these 'pre-complaints'. Some weeks, they sort out more than 60% of complaints without the need to record them. However, we keep a separate searchable record of them and watch for trends, so lessons can be learnt and we need to know if the same officer is being complained about repeatedly.

The Complaints Service Advisors have made this a success. The system is as good as the people who run it and ours are superb. They know the systems, they can navigate around quickly and efficiently and they are customer driven. They know that their job is to try to resolve the issues and get satisfaction for the complainant, whilst noting any lessons to be learned for police.

In times of austerity we were determined that the new system would be no additional cost to the force. In fact it will be a huge saver.

The public of Northumbria appear to welcome the change. In a recent survey, 92% of all complainants were happy with how their issue was dealt with by the Complaints Service Advisors – with 85% thinking the team could not have done more. In the early days they resolved around 35% of all complaints, we now regularly hit 50% plus. In the week of writing this article, the team had dealt with 63% of complaints. It continues to evolve; we have introduced home visits or meeting complainants at a local venue with which they feel comfortable.

If a case is likely to result in misconduct or gross misconduct proceedings, it is passed on immediately by the Complaints Service Advisors so that Professional Standards Department do not lose the 'golden hour' for investigation. In these serious or more complex cases the agent will monitor it and ensure that the complainant knows timescales and is kept informed as the investigation progresses.

This retains a personal contact so complainants are never dealing with 'a faceless organisation' and always have a channel of communication for questions or for reassurance.

The achievements by the Triage Team are having a positive effect on the Professional Standards Department which now has a demanding delivery plan. Like the triage system, all complainants are contacted within 24 hours and we aim to investigate and deal with at least half of all these serious cases in less than 50 days. Police officers also appreciate the system, recognising that the public have a quick and easy way to make complaints. Allegations of incivility, impoliteness and intolerance have dropped by 43% since last year.

At the opposite end of the process, I have appointed an Independent Scrutiny Panel of members of the public, to dip sample the cases which go beyond triage. We are very confident of the representative nature, the inquisitive approach and the high level of competence of the seven people who were selected by interview from those who volunteered. The very first thing they did was to meet with the Head of Professional Standards Department to say what they expected, as members of the public from a good police complaints system. They then dip sampled a dozen investigations to see whether they came up to that standard. They tell the Head of Professional Standards Department face to face what they have found and discuss with me, every few months trends concerns and improvements. We have more work to do but we see less defensiveness. Fresh eyes can throw a lot of light on the workings of an inward looking organisation.

A key objective is to learn lessons from this work and make changes as we move forward. We need to understand why people complain, improve our services to match and make a difference. Analysis of complaints will improve our understanding of what concerns local people, potentially informing future priorities for the Police and Crime Plan. We can also identify good practice to share across the force.

Northumbria is on the right path and I know we will continue to see improvements. The public will become more confident in the complaints system, the police officers will realise that times are changing and they need to work for customer care. It is all about turning potential enemies into much needed – and much valued – friends.

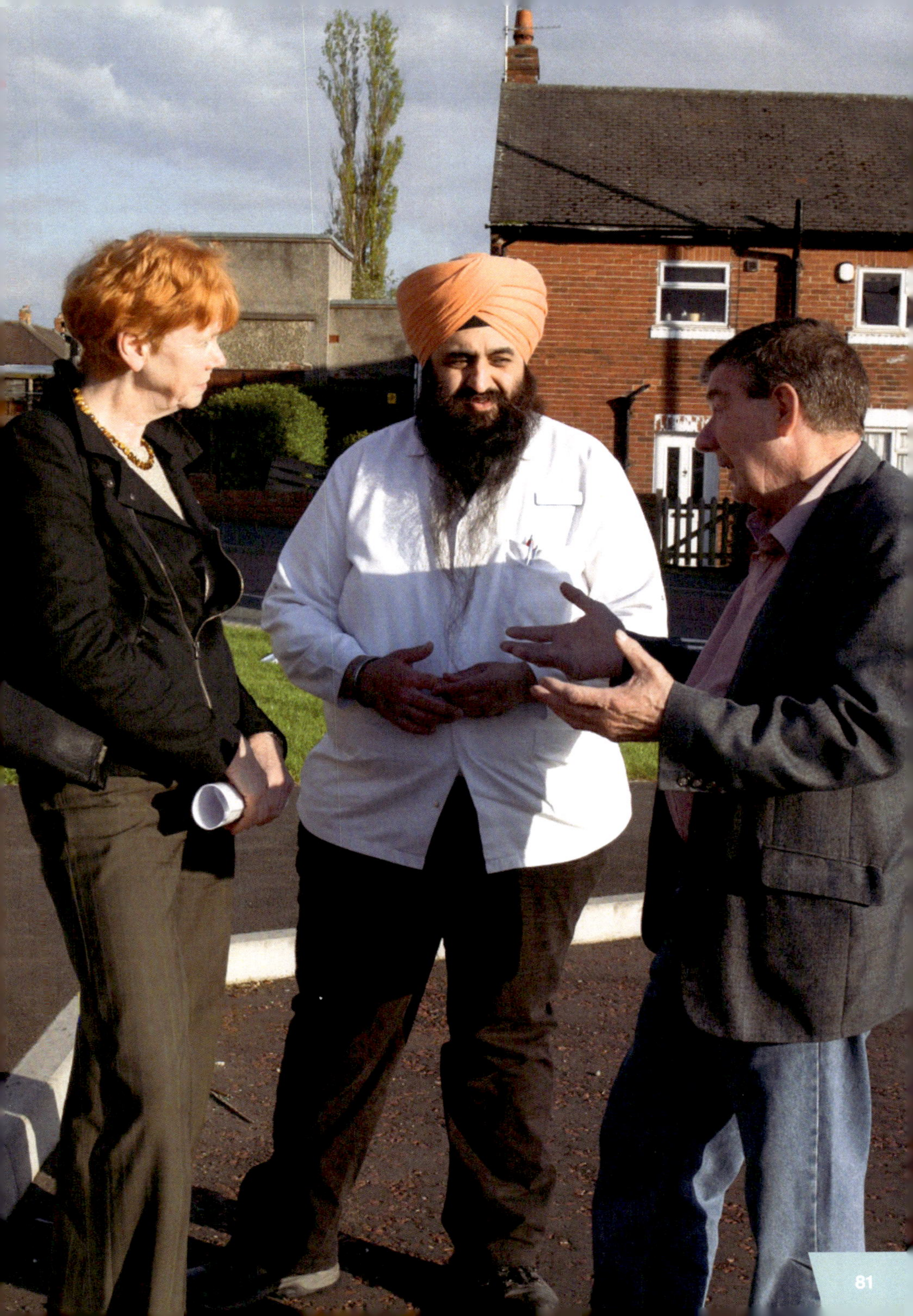

"Overwhelmingly of concern was the length of time it had taken for each case to proceed from charge to trial, with more than one over a year old. Such delays must be intolerable to defendants, complainants and families alike, and are beyond what is reasonable."

08
SEEING IS BELIEVING: NORTHUMBRIA'S COURT OBSERVERS

Police and the Crown Prosecution Service have worked hard, in recent years, to give confidence to victims of rape and sexual assault that they will receive sympathetic treatment and professional investigations. Complaints are going up but even as they do, convictions for rape are falling. Last year 61% of rape complaints resulted in a conviction, this year the figure is 55%.

Yet it is believed that 85% of rape victims still do not come forward, reportedly deterred by fear of not being believed and particularly by the courts' reputation for putting the victim last. Attacks on sexual reputation, scrutiny of what she was wearing, why she didn't struggle, why she reported it late and who she's had sex with before are all thought to be frequent features of cross examination. Rape support groups speak of trials where victims have felt raped all over again. They know of tragic events like the suicide of Frances Andrade after being cross-examined about her former music teacher, later convicted of sexually abusing her. 43% of a sample of victims who had given evidence felt it had not been worthwhile.

Whilst reporting sexual abuse can help people to find non-criminal justice support to cope and recover, it is critically important to convict sex offenders, who are often serial rapists and a threat to public safety.

Clearly the court process affects convictions but it also greatly influences police decisions about which future cases are likely to succeed. It will be no coincidence that the fall in convictions has resulted in a fall in the number of cases passed on to the Crown Prosecution Service. With that downward spiral in progress, complainants' confidence is not likely to get higher.

Extraordinarily, despite all this concern on an increasingly high-profile issue, nobody is scrutinising the courts. There is no inspectorate to match Her Majesty's Inspectors of Constabulary and the Crown Prosecution Service Inspectorate. Judges, Court Service, Probation, Witness Service and in-court equipment all play a role. Are the courts fair, are they competent, are they efficient, do they serve the public well; in particular in these most sensitive rape cases? In Northumbria we have set up a panel of citizen observers to watch and see. The Northumbria Police and Crime Commissioner's new volunteer Crown Court Observers scheme has now watched 27 trials.

As Police and Crime Commissioner in the locality I advertised for volunteers, with an impressive response; excellent applications who interviewed brilliantly; health professionals, academics, probation service, social workers, a retired court legal adviser and me, a criminal QC by trade. Thoroughly trained by the Crown Prosecution Service, they observe in pairs answering a matrix of questions which follow the trial process from beginning to end. They are neutral well informed and there to observe, offering a primary source of information to drive change and spread good practice. If they have seen it happening, it has happened.

My credentials are my duty under the Police Reform and Social Responsibility Act 2011 not only to secure efficient and effective policing, but to work with the criminal justice agencies to make an efficient and effective justice system too. In April 2015 Police and Crime Commissioners gained responsibility for victim services and compliance with the Code of Practice for Victims of Crime.

Judges are rightly jealous of their independence, though judicial independence does not equate to freedom from scrutiny and our local judiciary have welcomed us into court. If we can get these cases tried optimally, other cases will also improve. Secretary of State for Justice Michael Gove has himself watched some abuse trials and has asked for our results.

So far, our observers have watched adult rape trials in Newcastle Crown Court for a full six months. On their list are questions about those frequently expressed concerns on the impact of rape myths. Trial judges have a batch of directions which allow them to explain to juries such issues as why victims do not usually complain about rape immediately. It is generally thought that if a person is raped, they will scream for help right away but the courts know, from hundreds of past cases, that that is not so. People suffer such guilt, shame and shock that they rarely tell anyone what has happened for some time. That can be a very important point to make when the defence is that she consented to sex and her delay in reporting shows that she has made the complaint up later.

It is not true either, that because the complainant wore provocative clothing he/she must have wanted sex; nor that since the complainant got drunk in male company, he/she must have been prepared for sex; nor that an attractive male does not need to rape; nor that a complainant in a relationship with the alleged attacker is likely to have consented; nor that rape does not take place without physical resistance from the victim and usually causes injury and it is not universally true either, that rape by a stranger is necessarily more traumatic than rape by someone the victim knew and trusted.

All of these myths were until recently powerful weapons used by defendants, unchallenged by the prosecution or the court and were therefore taken to be true by juries. They played a key role in what was then an even lower conviction rate and there is little doubt that they continue to feature in the thinking of people who have never experienced sexual abuse either personally or by acquaintance and feature too, in the public discourse around rape. For some time judges themselves were trained to understand that these were prejudices and not truths and were finally given model directions, framed by the Judicial College, to enable them to pass on that understanding to juries.

Clearly the sought-after impact of these directions was to banish those prejudices from every part of a rape trial. However the judge does not sum up the case until the very end. Our observers have seen rape myths used liberally in cross examination, sometimes dramatically and they doubt that the wise words of the judge in summing up, sometimes several days later, are sufficient to neutralise their effect. Some judges use their advanced knowledge of a case to draw the jury's attention to myths that might come into play and to warn about them at the start of the trial. Those judges then typically intervene if the defence attempt to deploy any myths and reiterate their warning as well as repeating the directions in summing up. The observers think that this is good practice, especially since these myths are deeply ingrained into public attitudes about rape and may take more than one warning to displace.

In earlier days, defendants in trials where the defence was consent, would seek to prejudice the jury by alleging that the complainant was 'a loose woman' who had had sex with many other people and similarly been willing to have sex with him. The law now prohibits this kind of allegation, unless the judge agrees, in a pre-trial hearing, that the questions are relevant in some way and not merely prejudicial. Observers saw this process bypassed in their very first trial with prejudicial material allowed in. Other observers saw material put in cross examination which they thought, by analogy with sexual accusations, was irrelevant but undermining for the complainant.

In trial 1, the defence suggested that the complainant was mentally sick and that the defendant had often said to her "you are too much at times and a nutcase".

In trial 4, the complainant was asked if she was 'flirty' and when she said 'no' told that people are different in drink and asked the same question again.

In trial 3, an observer reported that the defence used stereotypes, citing the girlfriend of a famous male who cut up his clothes when she was jealous and asked if she was a 'bunny boiler' referring to a film where a woman kills her ex-boyfriend's pet when he is unfaithful.

In trial 5, the jury were told of "photographs taken from social media showing her exposing her breasts".

Decisions on the relevance of material such as this are determined by the trial judge and the observers have decided to compile a list of what they regard as worrying examples. It will be forwarded to all the judges as food for thought. The observers thought that preferable to appearing to criticise individuals about matter on which there is scope for genuine disagreement.

Independent Sexual Violence Advisers are professional support workers who help rape complainants, often over a lengthy

Newcastle Crown Court

period of time, both with practical issues and liaising with police and the courts. Our observers saw that they were rarely allowed to accompany the complainant when s/he gave evidence and instead there would be a volunteer from the Court-based Witness Service present. That would be a virtual stranger, much less of a support than an Independent Sexual Violence Adviser and was simultaneously a waste of the Independent Sexual Violence Adviser resource, since she would sit in the public gallery watching. When we raised this in our first meeting with the senior judges, it became clear that this was a simple communications issue. They thought that few barristers would know what an Independent Sexual Violence Adviser is and they appreciated that Independent Sexual Violence Advisers, themselves, have no means of asking the court if they can be with their client. It was agreed that we should ask the crown to get prosecution barristers to identify the Independent Sexual Violence Adviser and to ask if she can accompany the complainant. Usually the trial judge would agree.

We do want to make clear that the judges were universally praised by the panel for their deployment of the 'myth-busting' directions to the jury in summing up and were congratulated on their supportive attitude to vulnerable complainants.

For many years, it has been a requirement that prosecution barristers introduce themselves to the complainant for conversation but in very few had such a meeting been arranged. Often therefore the complainant would come to court without having any acquaintance with anyone from the trial team. Tyneside Rape Crisis staff made clear to us that such meetings are very important as confidence building exercises and the Crown Prosecution Service have undertaken to reinforce the need to formally arrange them.

In 3 cases jurors fell asleep in court and were not woken for some time. This somewhat cartoonish situation surprised and worried the observers, in particular where there were members of the complainant's family in the public gallery.

Overwhelmingly of concern was the length of time it had taken for each case to proceed from charge to trial, with more than one over a year old. Such delays must be intolerable to defendants, complainants and families alike, and are beyond what is reasonable.

The issues here are examples of the work the Observers have

begun. They can only pass on what they find, watch for change and speak more loudly and more widely if it does not occur. Their aim is to increase understanding between the courts, victims of sex crimes and the public by improving process where necessary and building complainants' confidence that they, as well as defendants, will be ensured a fair and unprejudiced hearing.

09
THE FIRST TRIAL: COURT OBSERVERS TELL THE STORY

On the first day of the trial, Durham Prison forgot to put the defendant, Mr Krovo onto their van and Newcastle Crown Court assembled at 10.30am to try someone who wasn't there. Not only was he absent but his defence statement, due months before, to disclose his version of events to the court, was also missing. He was charged with rape forcing his wife to have unwanted sex on numerous occasions as their marriage broke down, and with finally doing so on 29th December 2013 before kicking her downstairs, when she called the police.

Judge Mountford's first words were about the delay. He was due to be hearing a case on Friday in the Court of Appeal and it was Tuesday already.

Where was the defendant? Where was the defence statement? And would the case definitely finish by Thursday?

Defence counsel said that the trouble was the defendant spoke Polish. He, personally, was busy, it was hard to get an interpreter to the prison so he hadn't had a chance to agree with his client what should be put in a defence statement.

This was the first trial for the Police and Crime Commissioner's new Court Observers. Volunteers would observe, in pairs, every adult rape trial in Newcastle Court from January to July 2015, filling in the answers to a list of questions about how well or how poorly the justice agencies were doing their job.

In the canteen, waiting for the van to go back for Mr Krovo, the observers ate their lunch, as the 15 members of the jury-in-waiting, summoned for the regulation 3 weeks service and being paid their loss of earnings, similarly ate their lunch at the Crown Court.

At 2.15pm, Mr Krovo sat in the dock with an interpreter. His counsel handed a defence statement to the judge with its ink still wet. It said that Mrs Krovo had had affairs with two work colleagues but he and she still had sex because they loved each other. "Now we are ready to go", his counsel said. But this was not the case. If he wanted to cross examine Mrs Krovo about adultery he should have applied for the consent of the judge to do so, weeks before.

In 1999, the Labour Government passed a law to stop the widespread practice in rape trials of suggesting that the complainant 'sleeps around' and is therefore likely to have consented to sex with the defendant. Since that date, allegations about sexual activity with other people can only be put to a rape victim in court if a judge decides in a preliminary hearing that they are relevant in some other way. Then, the complainant will be told that she will be asked about them and she, in turn, can tell the prosecution if there are any witnesses to say that the allegations are untrue.

Inexplicably, in this case, the prosecution did not argue either about the lateness of this application or about its merit. She simply conceded that the defence could cross examine the victim about the alleged affairs. The judge had little option but to agree.

The observers wrote:

"What was the relevance of whether Mrs Krovo had had affairs, if he said they had sex because they loved each other? How would her infidelity show she consented to sex with him?"

So far, so bad. But Mrs Krovo has also been waiting at court all day. When she is called to take the oath, she will not know that there will be allegations of adultery and has no chance to tell the prosecution if the men in question will give evidence to deny it. The defence has ignored the rules; the prosecution has let prejudice roll in. But worse is yet to come. The prosecution now admits that the police interview with the defendant is such a poor recording it cannot be played and that there is only one low quality photograph of the injuries Mr Krovo caused to the complainant.

The observers, noting that Mrs Krovo's case has been further weakened by poor quality evidence gathering, wrote:

"If I had been a relative of the victim sitting in the public gallery I would have had a severe lack of confidence in the proceedings."

Her evidence, videoed shortly after the event, was played to the jury. On it she said that she had wanted to leave her husband because he drank, did not work, forced her to have sex, and accused her of having affairs with every man she knew. She had looked for a new home for herself and the children and had offered to buy him a ticket back to Poland but he would not leave and kept telling her he still loved her. The video was exactly a year old the day the jury saw it.

She was cross examined across a live television link to a room outside the court, a common practice to save the victim the stress of speaking about embarrassing events from the witness box.

The defence barrister's questions were allegations - that Mrs Krovo drank uncontrollably, that her husband called her 'crazy' and that she was having affairs. She denied them all.

The observers wrote:

"He tried to discredit her by suggesting she had affairs and was a bad mother as she sometimes drank alcohol. The alleged affairs have nothing to do with the rapes."

The barrister then produced a transcript of incoming and outgoing texts downloaded from Mr Krovo's phone when he was arrested, which included messages from him to her and vice-versa. The barrister suggested that affectionate texts such as "You will be forever in my heart" were from her to him but she denied it. Mrs Krovo had never seen the transcript nor read the texts since they were sent in November 2013.

The barrister became confused about which texts were sent from Mr Krovo's phone and which were received. "Who texted who to go to Tesco?" he asked. One of the jurors fell asleep.

He finally suggested that a text "How RU darling?" came to Mr Krovo's phone from her and a text "We can make this work" came from

Mr Krovo's phone the next day, so one of these two loving texts must have come from her. She disagreed, pointing out that they both had pre-paid phones and frequently swopped them so whoever needed it had the one with most credit. That answer meant that this line of questioning was futile because all the affectionate texts could have come from him to her, as she said. The court adjourned for a break. The juror woke up having missed very little.

The observers wrote:

"You could see most of the jury had switched off or were irritated, the prosecution should never have let her be questioned on the transcript without reading it first, she would probably have said at the start that the phones were swopped about and prevented a lot of time wasting and confusion"

The observers saw the police officer in charge of the case and asked why the two male work colleagues and the Krovo children were not prosecution witnesses. She shrugged, because she hadn't known the defence was about adultery until the previous day.

The observers wrote:

"Why didn't she get her barrister to ask the court for time to interview these witnesses or do them overnight, so they could come to court tomorrow? How have the police allowed the defence to be so late with these allegations and then done nothing to respond to them?"

After the break, Mr Krovo gave evidence through the interpreter. He said his wife had had affairs and tried to leave him for her first lover; she drank constantly. He looked after the children and bought her vodka to keep the peace. They often had sex because they loved each other, the affectionate messages on the texts were mutual.

In cross examination he denied that he was possessive and said that his wife 'liked sex', and that was the end of the evidence.

The prosecution barrister argued in her closing speech that if Mrs Krovo was telling the truth, he was guilty.

The defence speech concentrated on the alleged affairs and hinted that she might have been so drunk when having sex with Mr Krovo that she thought he had raped her. He said because she denied these affairs it meant she was a liar so they could believe she was lying about being raped. However he accepted that whether she had affairs had in itself no bearing on whether this was rape.

The observers noted:

"The defence barrister went on and on about the affairs but admitted that they were irrelevant to the issue of whether he raped her and only put in to discredit her. Letting these in was a huge error by the prosecution barrister."

The judge summarised the evidence and warned the jury against drawing on common rape myths. He told them not to speculate about witnesses who hadn't been called but made no comment on the relevance/irrelevance of the allegations of adultery to the question of rape.

The jury retired; they found the defendant not guilty.

The observers wrote:

"The delay was terrible and the reasons given poor. This cannot be the first case where an interpreter is needed and the defendant was in prison. The late arrival of the defendant, I cannot believe a whole defendant interview was no good. The delay in the defence statement, no witnesses for the prosecution, one poor photo of her injuries, the texts transcripts in the wrong order, phones not identified correctly, cross examination unfair, long rambles, no questions, mocking and demeaning.

Judge made some effort re myths but he was needed elsewhere shortly and just wanted the jury out as quickly as possible."

These observations seem to add support to what Michael Gove the new Secretary of State for Justice told this year's Conservative party conference:

"Our criminal justice system is still blighted by inefficiencies, delays and injustices"

"Northumbria Police targets sexual exploitation and works with others to protect people who are vulnerable whether through age or otherwise."

10
PROJECT SANCTUARY: TARGETING SEXUAL EXPLOITATION AND WORKING WITH OTHERS TO PROTECT THE VULNERABLE

Written by Vera Baird QC and Steve Ashman, Chief Constable of Northumbria Police

At the Coalition Government's Child Sexual Exploitation Summit at 10 Downing Street, on 3rd March 2015, Prime Minister Cameron said complaints of Child Sexual Exploitation had increased nationally by 57% in eighteen months and that there was a continuing upward trend. As with nationally, Northumbria shows a similar upward trend.

These figures do not demonstrate a significant increase in the experience of such crimes. Rather, they represent increased reporting to the police of sexual exploitation that had previously remained unreported. Much of this increase in reporting can be attributed to the work carried out by police forces, together with partner agencies, nationwide, since the scandals identified in Rotherham and those arising from what have been termed 'celebrity' sex abuse trials. Such work has seen significant investment, including specific emphasis towards hard-to-reach victim communities, leading to increasing confidence and increased reporting.

Sooner or later the Government will have to acknowledge the need for further funding, consistent with those increases in reporting, for police services, criminal justice agencies and charities involved in supporting victims and bringing perpetrators to justice. It is believed there may be a cross-departmental bid into the Chancellor of the Exchequers next review of future spending (the Comprehensive Spending Review) due on November 25th, for such a budget.

However, inter-agency work also needs to go further, by unearthing the presence of sexual exploitation wherever it continues to be under-reported. This type of offending often remains hidden, partly because it can involve victims who are vulnerable in such a way that they do not recognise they are being abused. Other victims do not trust the police and, of course, sexual abuse is, in itself very difficult to discuss. The revelations arising from Rotherham demonstrate no area can be sure that serious sexual exploitation does not exist within its boundaries and nobody can say they truly understand the prevalence of this particularly invidious form of offending.

In Northumbria, Operation Sanctuary is a police-led, multi-agency operation, which began its work in January 2014, to target criminal behaviour by men who commit sexual offences against vulnerable women and children. It came into being as a result of a complaint of different criminal activity which, almost tangentially, gave a hint that organised sexual exploitation may be occurring. Whilst the operation remains very much 'ongoing' it is developing from a dedicated, specific operation focussing on a particular time and place, to becoming a proven, strategic method of identifying and pursuing this type of criminality so as to achieve a sustainable, widespread approach to safeguarding victims.

Now called Project Sanctuary, the approach adopts the widest range of policing techniques, both overt and covert, to proactively identify and engage with those who are identified as potential complainants and victims. The arising investigations are supported by significant offender disruption activity and extensive community engagement. Police investigation teams are supported by partners such as social workers from Children's and Adults Social Care, voluntary staff from the Children's Society, Barnardo's, Changing Lives and Health.

We know from this work that trafficking offences are on the increase and if we are to identify and apprehend criminals that prey on the vulnerable we will need to apportion more police time and resources towards this type of offending; we will also need to work with other forces at a regional and potentially national level. Northumbria Police, Durham Constabulary and Cleveland Police are all undertaking investigations into sexual exploitation and child sexual exploitation, although the Northumbria investigation is the most significant in magnitude at this time. Intelligence sharing by the North East Regional Special Operations Unit (a jointly funded unit with key responsibility for serious and organised crime) has identified subjects who are operating at a regional level as well as victims who are being trafficked across regional boundaries.

The offences under investigation undoubtedly arise from sexual exploitation of vulnerable victims. Our clearly held belief is that vulnerability is the common factor amongst victims, albeit the nature of such vulnerability varies. There is certainly a high level of vulnerability associated with young age but it is also apparent that people are being subjected to abuse in consequence of vulnerabilities arising from learning disabilities, previous personal hardship and/or earlier exploitation, low self-esteem and also from intoxication with drink or drugs. People in these categories whom have achieved eighteen years of age can still remain vulnerable to being groomed, trafficked and exploited. Work with safeguarding partners therefore spans not only children but also those in transition to young adulthood.

The Sanctuary methodology has emerged through a number of smaller operations such as Operation Jupiter, an investigation into sexual exploitation based mainly within the Sunderland area. To date this operation has achieved a ten year sentence for one man for rape and sexual assault. Several investigations also remain on-going, some of which already involve criminal proceedings with others likely to do so.

Operation Shelter is a similar investigation, although this operation is mainly confined to the west end of Newcastle upon Tyne. Thus far the operation has convicted one man for the rape of a 14 year old girl, resulting in a ten year term of imprisonment, a second man for sexual activity with a 14 year old girl, resulting in a six year term of imprisonment and the conviction of a third man, who received an eight year sentence for a number of sexual offences involving children, some as young as 10 years of age.

Operation Shield is a force-wide operation focussing on the sexual offending activities of taxi drivers and bogus taxi drivers. Thus far the operation has resulted in the

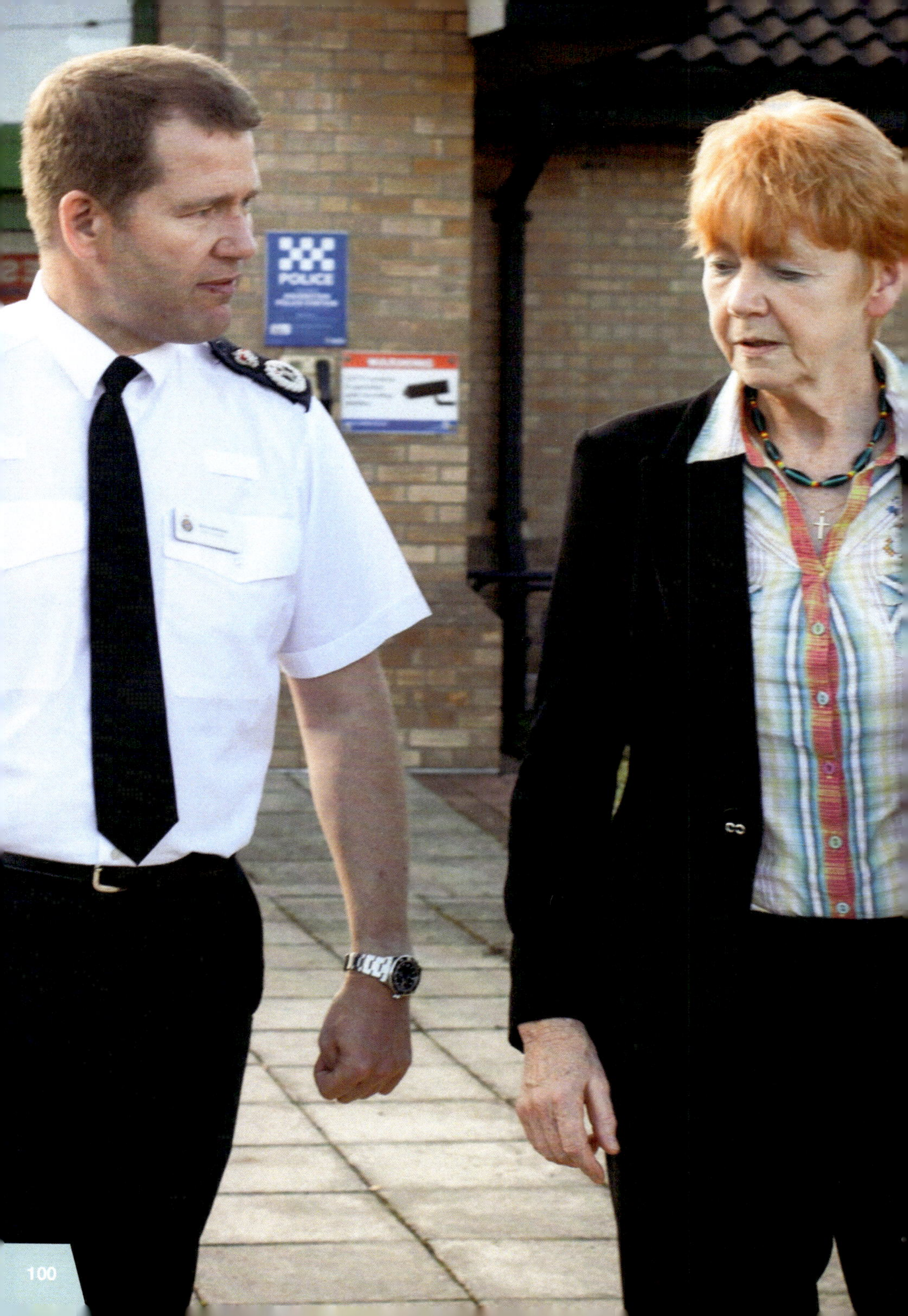
POLICE

convictions of three men, all of whom have received substantial terms of imprisonment. Partnership work has been imperative in this area, with local authority taxi licensing involved in all investigations and a number of subjects having licences removed resulting in consequence of both criminal charges and intelligence sharing. The majority of taxi drivers have joined police in tackling abuse by others with many undertaking training themselves to help identify vulnerability.

A number of covert operations have also been conducted to target subjects involved in sexual exploitation and drug supply. One man is currently awaiting sentence, having been convicted of conspiracy to supply Class A, B and C drugs and possession of a firearm. Evidence of drug supply has also been gathered, using covert techniques, against thirty additional subjects, some of whom are also believed to be involved in sexual exploitation offences; charging decisions are awaited from the Crown Prosecution Service. An recent inspection, carried out by the Office of the Surveillance Commissioners, identified Northumbria Police as being at the forefront of covert work in the area of sexual exploitation; in respect of both undercover deployment and surveillance activity.

The link between the supply of controlled drugs and sexual exploitation is significant, partly because an identified model of organised sexual exploitation in Northumbria, as elsewhere in the country, is through a series of 'party scenarios'. Older men will groom younger vulnerable women, becoming their admiring 'boyfriend', giving them material gifts, cocaine, cannabis and alcohol and will take them to party 'sessions'; whereupon more drink and drugs will be provided and the victims exploited by the 'friends' of the 'boyfriend'. Sometimes women are drunk or drugged to a level of unconsciousness before being raped and abused. Often they will go on to take drugs on a self-medicating basis, as a means of coping with multiple abuse experiences, giving the 'boyfriend' drug supplier ever stronger leverage over them.

These operations and related intelligence have made clear that the exploitation problem is bigger than the force originally thought. Evidence of new conspiracies is continuing to emerge and produce further lines of inquiry. Although there are paedophiles involved, exploitation locally is not confined to children, nor is it exclusively about a crisis in the care system; although many victims are subject to local authority care and are often repeat runaways. Vulnerability is the one binding factor.

Local authority buy-in and assistance is pivotal, with co-located multi-agency teams identified as being the key way forward. Other professionals have been co-located with police at the core of the investigational hub so that dynamic sharing of information between partners can assist safeguarding efforts. A non-police led victim strategy, involving social services and the voluntary sector, is essential to securing trust and confidence with potential complainants, many of whom are anti-police or afraid of the consequences for themselves of involvement with the Criminal Justice System.

Marketing of the project in the local community is essential to maintaining both confidence in the police response and to collecting intelligence. In the original territorial span of Operation Shelter, the neighbourhood policing teams were taken away from all other duties for a period of time to sustain the marketing project and to reassure the public.

This year, Northumbria Police succeeded in obtaining a Police Innovation Fund Grant, from the Home Office, which identifies a response to these pressing and important issues and is designed to build on the success of the earlier and on-going operations. The key elements to the bid are resulting in further important innovations in how Northumbria tackles sexual exploitation.

This includes the establishment of two multi-agency operational teams, one covering the north of the force and the other the south, to tackle child exploitation, vulnerability and modern day slavery. The teams are co-located within non-police premises to establish community 'hubs' that will take a victim-based approach in keeping with good practice identified during Project Sanctuary. The intention of co-location within a hub arrangement is to bring together Children and Adult Social Care Services, Healthcare staff, the Police and a broad range of third sector organisations and partners to build on 'what works' within Project Sanctuary. Both voluntary and non-voluntary organisations will be represented, and the hubs will each include four dedicated Social Workers; thereby achieving representation from each of the local authority areas in the force area.

In addition to those organisations occupying co-located space within each hub, SCARPA (the Children's

Society) will work alongside embedded Missing From Home Co-ordinators and the Local Children's Safeguarding Board group that focuses on missing, sexually exploited or trafficked groups to reduce the numbers/frequency of children going missing from home. As well as dealing with matters in their own right, the hubs will link directly with Victims First Northumbria, the local victim care unit. This and deployment of the Commissioner's share of the Ministry of Justice Victims Fund will develop and provide additional opportunities for providing bespoke services to victims in a timely and effective way; services which will remain with each referred victim until they determine that they themselves have been sufficiently assisted to cope and to recover from the impact of crime. As criminal trials approach an enormous amount of support is required to sustain victims. The support process can be integral with intelligence gathering, much of the detailed information giving rise to a local picture comes from the victims, with every name or place mentioned being taken into consideration.

The new funding has also provided, for the very first time, two new roles; a new Child Sexual Exploitation Social Work Co-ordinator role to work with sexually exploited children and a new Sexual Exploitation Social Work Co-ordinator role to work with sexually exploited adults. These roles will oversee and co-ordinate social work activity across individual local authority boundaries.

Dedicated Investigative Units are driven by the work from the hubs to target identified perpetrators. These dedicated units consist of mixed teams, each comprising eighteen experienced police officers (3 Detective Sergeants and 15 Detective Constables) and four experienced Social Workers who will conduct investigations jointly. The investigative units are in police premises and are totally separate to the community based hubs.

The entire activity of the hubs and their dedicated investigative units will also be enhanced by the use of state-of-the-art technology enabled by funding achieved via this bid. The use of location-based social media monitoring software together with investigative activity regarding use of the internet will be used to drive preventative and enforcement activity. Additionally, a computerised application, an 'App', will be developed to create a contemporary, widely accessible interface to share and receive safeguarding information with those susceptible to exploitation, particularly young people.

In addition we have held a workshop together with the three regional forces and the National Crime Agency, who have already advised on Project Sanctuary. The objective of the workshop was to share investigative strategies and tactical knowledge and to quality assure the intelligence links and development across the region in respect of sexual exploitation.

We know that to be successful within the arena of sexual exploitation investigation requires an effective partnership working between the police and a number of partner agencies. The most important of these partner agencies is Children's and Adults Social Care. The ongoing work between the Operation Shelter team and Newcastle Children's and Adults Social Care is an excellent example of an effective partnership within the arena of sexual exploitation.

This joined-up working has not only assisted with the investigative process but more importantly has allowed support to be delivered to significant numbers of young girls and adults who have been affected by sexual exploitation. A number of areas of best practice have been identified from this partnership activity. A further local authority workshop has been held across all 12 regional local authorities in the Northumbria Durham and Cleveland areas encompassing both Children's Social Care and Adults Social Care. Key features included how to maximise safeguarding opportunities for those most at risk by applications for secure placement and other joint approaches for those who do not reach the threshold for secure accommodation, involving the investigative team in that work. It also covered sexual exploitation assessment within Social Care and Policing and how to recognise the signs of sexual exploitation through the use of social media and a review of social care practice amongst Social Workers allowing better work with these victims.

Northumbria's bold multi-agency and regional approach to sexual exploitation directs resources at the frontline of policing to tackle a growing problem that we still need to learn more about. By working with others national and locally we can, as recent convictions show, stem this tide of abuse and criminality.

As we go forward we are increasing our input into education which will be essential to prevent the next generation of offenders and victims coming through. We succeeded in securing a further Police Innovation Fund grant in order to develop a Centre of Excellence in a joint Fire and Rescue run hub called

SafetyWorks! where traditional work with young people on issues such as road and fire safety will become secondary to smart interactive learning about identification and resistance to sexual grooming, the meaning of consent and good personal relationships.

Protecting the vulnerable from gangs who prey on them must be at the forefront of priorities in policing in Northumbria. As Chief Constable and Police and Crime Commissioner we speak with one voice on this. Project Sanctuary is at the top of our priorities.

"What I remember most about emotional abuse is that it's like being put in a box... Maybe you think it's a treasure box at first: you're in there because you're special. Soon the box starts to shrink. Every time you touch the edges there is an 'argument'. So you try to make yourself fit. You curl up, become smaller, quieter, remove the excessive, offensive parts of your personality – you begin to notice lots of these. You eliminate people and interests, change your behaviour. But still the box gets smaller. You think it's your fault.... You don't yet understand that you will never, ever be tiny enough to fit, or silent enough to avoid a row – because they aren't rows. If you're lucky – like my friend and me – you get to leave the situation. I'm not sure whether you ever completely escape the experience."

Lauren Laverne, Observer, 7.09.14

11
PROGRESS AGAINST DOMESTIC ABUSE THROUGH UNDERSTANDING COERCIVE CONTROL

Section 76 of the Serious Crime Act 2015, passed in March this year, creates for the first time ever a criminal offence of domestic abuse. It is punishable by a maximum sentence of 5 years imprisonment. The offence is called 'controlling and coercive behaviour in an intimate or family relationship' and by putting those words into legislation, the concept of coercive control as a continuing pattern of behaviour is brought to the fore.

In the violence against women sector the centrality in domestic abuse of coercive and controlling behaviour has long been understood but it remains almost unknown to those outside. Now it is elevated as an important thing to understand in order to implement the new law. In fact understanding the concept is likely to prove at least as important for tackling the epidemic of domestic abuse as the criminal offence.

Prior to the coercive control offence, there was no means of reflecting, in criminality, conduct going beyond individual acts, most commonly assaults of differing gravities. Police would attend and if there was a black eye would charge the perpetrator with an assault causing bodily harm or if there was a cut perhaps with an offence of wounding. What underlay those injuries and the multiple earlier events that officers will have been called to before, has not been seen as part of domestic abuse. The perception has been that troublesome couples frequently fall out and one gets violent to the other, she calls the police but when the crisis is over won't press charges. She will resolve herself back into her domestic situation until the next incident of domestic abuse occurs. Courts have a similar perspective. These criminal justice agencies exist to implement the law. Until now there has only been law to deal with episodic violence and so why or how would they learn that episodic violence is not the true nature of domestic abuse, which is coercive control.

There is a helpful background of stalking law, strengthened in 2012, which recognises the need to capture an underlying 'course of conduct' which would cause any 'reasonable person' experiencing it to suffer 'serious alarm or distress'. Classically, a fixated stranger is regarded as impacting on the victim in this way. In fact, many stalkers are former partners, carrying on very similar behaviour to that which they use during their relationship and with the same intention.

The domestic abuse offence defines controlling behaviour as a range of acts designed to make a person subordinate to and/or dependent on their abuser by isolating them from sources of support, exploiting their resources and capacities for personal gain, depriving them of the means needed for independence, resistance and escape and regulating their everyday behaviour. Coercive behaviour is an act or a pattern of acts of assault, threats, humiliation and intimidation or other abuse that is used to harm, punish, or frighten their victim.

Learned literature, the testimony of victims and the experience of a range of charities shows typical coercive and controlling tactics used in domestic abuse.

Isolation

This often begins very early in the relationship, before other forms of abuse. It is controlling what the victim does, who they see and who they speak to, limiting their involvement with the outside world because that can be both a source of support for the victim and of challenge to the authority/control of the abusive partner.

Emotional abuse

Often next to develop this consists of putting the individual down, making them feel bad about themselves, calling them names, humiliating them in front of others. It boosts the control of the abusive partner by undermining self-esteem. It will focus on whatever the victim values about themselves most. So if they value their intelligence, they may be told they are stupid.

Minimising, denying and blaming

When physical violence is used, the abusive partner will need to control the victim's reaction to it – by minimising what they have done, 'it was only a slap', denying they did it, 'I didn't mean to hurt you', or shifting responsibility for the assault onto her, 'If you hadn't done X it wouldn't have happened at all'.

Intimidation

Once the possibility of physical/sexual violence has been established, intimidation can be enough to keep the victim in line. Police officers will often see punch marks in walls and doors which are there to send the message to the victim 'I chose to miss you, this time, but next time I might not'.

Using children to control the victim

Children will be present meaning they are in the same room, the next room or upstairs in 9 out of 10 incidents, and it can be a very damaging experience, as child protection law has recognised since 2002 children are often also used to keep the victim in line. For instance, the partner of a local woman with an autistic child who couldn't cope with loud noise or shouting would bring him to the victim whilst he assaulted her knowing that this child, in particular, would not cope with the assault and that she would not cope with this particular child being there. Contact with children is also used after separation as a means to find out about her new life so that he can demonstrate that he knows what she is doing and that she can't escape even though she lives elsewhere.

Financial abuse/control

Is very common in domestic abuse because controlling finances is to control options. Many victims do not know that refuge and other services are free at the point of delivery and will assume that having no money means that they can't pay for help and so have no way out.

Threats

To abandon them, to remove a child, to report them to children services are used to reinforce day to day control over them. Threatening suicide is another such way, common at the point of separation; when the abusive partner is beginning to lose control over the victim.

Male privilege

Research from the recent Project Mirabal, a project about perpetrator programmes, shows that domestic abusers use traditional ideas to justify their behaviour such as an intention to protect her against bad influences (usually from her friends and family), and that a man is understandably possessive about a partner he loves. The coercive control framework does not downplay the fact that women also assault partners but there is nowhere any clear evidence of similar entrapment of men by women due to coercive control.

It is not widely understood that separation increases the risk of serious harm to a victim and will not automatically end coercive and controlling behaviour. Courts, in particular, have a history of seeing abuse in the context of the heated dynamics of a breaking relationship which cool when one party leaves the other. Complaints of abuse, for instance in applications for parenting and contact are often seen as raking up history and certainly no evidence that a perpetrator is not 'a good father' despite the legislative acceptance, in 2002, that children, are harmed by witnessing abuse.

The true position is that separation is a highly dangerous time because she is effectively taking control back. The partner may send fond messages such as 'I can change' but if that fails more threatening messages will follow. The level of violence and harassment will intensify as the perpetrator senses his loss of grip. He will use what he knows of the victim's routines to follow or intercept her, will contact her friends and will wait for her at their children's school or her place of work.

At least one third of all domestic abuse incidents occur after separation and, very significantly, so do many domestic violence deaths. Our conferences about Workplace Domestic Abuse Champions feature the story of Fiona, now a successful businesswoman, whose violent partner was so persistent that she feels her life was saved only by her employer moving her to a remote branch office where he couldn't find her. Refuges frequently need to accommodate women far away from a partner who will not relinquish their abusive hold on their victim.

The impact of these behaviours is to produce fear not only of particular incidents but also an ongoing or 'chronic' fear, often over periods of years (Pain, 2012). It is living an entire life 'walking on egg shells'. Many victims restrict their own activities and interactions with others in the vain hope that this will keep them safe. Family and friends can experience the impact of what are nonetheless coerced behaviours as hurtful and commonly attribute blame to the victim, adding to her isolation. Similarly, police who experience antagonism from an apparent victim think that she is behaving badly of her own free will when she will be terrified that they will make her disclose the true picture, earning her renewed punishment from the perpetrator.

Understanding this concept is urgent as well as necessary, given the legal changes because research shows that coercive control is a more accurate predictor of domestic homicide than physical violence. Many women have died at the hands of partners with no evidence of prior assault but much of highly controlling behaviour. Its emergence will be hugely welcomed by women's sector practitioners who have struggled in the past to overcome the 'incidentalism' of the Criminal Justice System and to get them to recognise that incidents are only a part of a larger systematic whole.

In a safeguarding context, a ruling of Lord Justice Munby (Re SA (Vulnerable Adult with Capacity: Marriage) [2006] 1 FLR 867 (Munby J)) recognised this problem when he saw a case for the court to protect a vulnerable adult who has the capacity to make their own decisions but is not free to do so due to coercive/controlling behaviour from another. This ruling hardly featured in safeguarding policy until the second edition of the LGA/ADASS guidance on 'Adult Safeguarding & Domestic Abuse' was published in 2015 but it may provide a useful authority to drive understanding of the disabling impact of typically controlling behaviour.

Appreciation is due to the work of Evan Stark, an American sociologist and expert court witness on domestic abuse who wrote a book in 2007 called 'Coercive Control: How Men Entrap Women in Personal Life' hugely influential in the States and which in the UK, fed into the thinking which underpinned the new offence.

Her Majesty's Inspectorate of Constabulary's report on the policing of domestic abuse ('Everyone's business: Improving the police response to domestic abuse, Her Majesty's Inspectorate of Constabulary, 2014') also set out the need for new understanding. In Northumbria Police, training has been developed with Wearside Women in Need, our largest refuge and outreach charity. It includes the following examples of how a controlling partner will try to manipulate the criminal justice agencies in different circumstances.

During the initial police response the perpetrator will often seek to take control of the situation by appearing friendly, calm and plausible. In 30% of domestic abuse assault cases reviewed by the Her Majesty's Inspectorate of Constabulary in 2014, the perpetrator tried to derail the investigation of him by making a counter-allegation against her. He will try to prevent access to the victim, children, family members and neighbours to impede evidence gathering in the important 'Golden Hour'.

Safety planning will be undermined. He will remove her phone or listen in and press her to retract. Officers need to build understanding with the victim, at the start. The introduction of DVSA cars (in chapter 5) is directed to getting police and experienced partners into one to one private contact with the victim to explore options and address their safety.

Managing risk victims are frequently too afraid to support police action, but nonetheless want the situation to change. They don't want to be the central or only plank of the investigation but need officers to understand coercive control so as to collect a wider body of evidence towards a prosecution which can take place with or without the victim. New tools such as body-worn cameras can assist.

The Crown Prosecution Service, the Magistracy and Judges equally need to be trained beyond the mechanics of the new offence into understanding coercive and controlling behaviour and the tactics used in domestic abuse. That will help to clarify what underlies retractions of victim complaints and the need for supportive evidence to give her confidence or even to allow the case to progress without her. Courts will appreciate that perpetrators of domestic abuse will frequently pose as victims and that their role includes identifying the primary aggressor. They will understand the serial nature of domestic abuse offending and can use evidence of previous bad conduct to show a continuing course of conduct, very different from the single incident trials which currently happen on a 'he said, she said' basis. They will understand too how controlling behaviours can play out even within the court building and its processes and will recognise the need for protection of the victim and deterrence of the perpetrator long after she has separated from him. Learning from the criminal courts will need to be spread to the family courts so that decision making about parenting and contact can also be done in full knowledge of the true nature of domestic abuse.

The next, now foreseeable, step will be to spread this understanding to the broader public so that they become aware of the coercive control typically exercised over victims who are often too undermined to help themselves and can only escape with the informed assistance of friends and family. A key step is to ensure, as we have with Northumbria Police, that training is given to all the agencies, by those from the domestic abuse sector who understand this concept in depth. It would be tragic if the criminal justice agencies' current lack of awareness of the nature of domestic abuse prevented them from seeing the need to understand it and led to a minimalist focus only on the legal meaning of the new law. The advent of the new domestic abuse offence, if it brings the concept of coercive control into popular consciousness, can be this century's best prospect of making domestic abuse the anathema it should be and a crime that everyone will wish to stamp out. We must not lose this opportunity.

"If the UK Government could decide what human rights to have or remove. It would empower other regimes around the world to dilute their human rights protections when they become inconvenient."

12
WE NEED OUR HUMAN RIGHTS – DISPELLING THE MYTHS

Little public information, complicated terminology and a plethora of similar names, such as the European Convention on Human Rights, the Human Rights Act and the Strasbourg Court means that unless they have had a specific need, few ordinary British people will know much about human rights.

Further, a mainly adverse press has generated innumerable myths to fill the gap, ironically, since a number of journalistic freedoms are attributable to human rights. The Government seizes on these myths and has arguably added a dash of xenophobia to persuade us that these European (foreign) rights are perverse and only help bad people against the good. They are wrong. We all need our human rights.

Ordinary people benefit hugely from the Human Rights Act. In Northumbria, as elsewhere, people have been able to use it to assert or protect their rights against bureaucracy or officialdom and against over-bearing, unfair or neglectful public authorities. Britain has had human rights since we helped to fashion the post war European Convention in 1951 but, for individuals, they were only enforceable by the costly and cumbersome process of going to the European Court in Strasbourg. That's why the Labour Government in 1998 published the document 'Bringing Our Rights Back Home' and passed the Human Rights Act. It empowers our British courts to directly enforce all the Convention rights, leaving the Strasbourg Court as an appeal court of last resort, whose judgements are given regard but which cannot strike down or change our laws.

Some examples show the ordinary day to day importance of the Human Rights Act.

Last June, the Supreme Court, the highest Court in England and Wales, found that the Government owed a duty of care to properly equip and train soldiers sent to war. The case was brought using the Human Rights Act by the families of several soldiers, who like some of our north eastern lads, were killed in battle in Iraq or Afghanistan. They argued their case to save other young military personnel from being exposed to excessive risk by being ill-equipped for action. They won a duty of care against the Ministry of Defence who have to provide troops with adequate protection and, the Court said, had failed to do so in these cases.

A one parent family which was made homeless was helped by the local council to find new accommodation for the two children but were refused similar help for the mother. The local law centre helped the family to take legal action against this decision, arguing that separating the children, one of whom is disabled, from their mother would breach their human right to private and family life.

An elderly couple were threatened with separation by their local social services department who wanted to move Mrs V to a care home that was too far away for Mr V and other members of the family to visit. Mr V successfully challenged this decision using the same right to private and family life which had helped the homeless family. The council had to place Mrs V somewhere which fulfilled her needs but was compatible with her remaining in touch with her family.

Another important benefit is that the Human Rights Act puts a duty on the state to protect people against breaches of key rights by other people. This is especially helpful for victims of crime. Two young women who were attacked by the London 'black cab rapist', John Worboys, successfully sued the Metropolitan Police for failing to investigate their complaints 'independently and impartially'. Police are part of the state machinery and have a duty to protect people's human right, under Article 3 of the Convention and the Human Rights Act not to suffer from inhuman or degrading treatment. Suffering rape or being

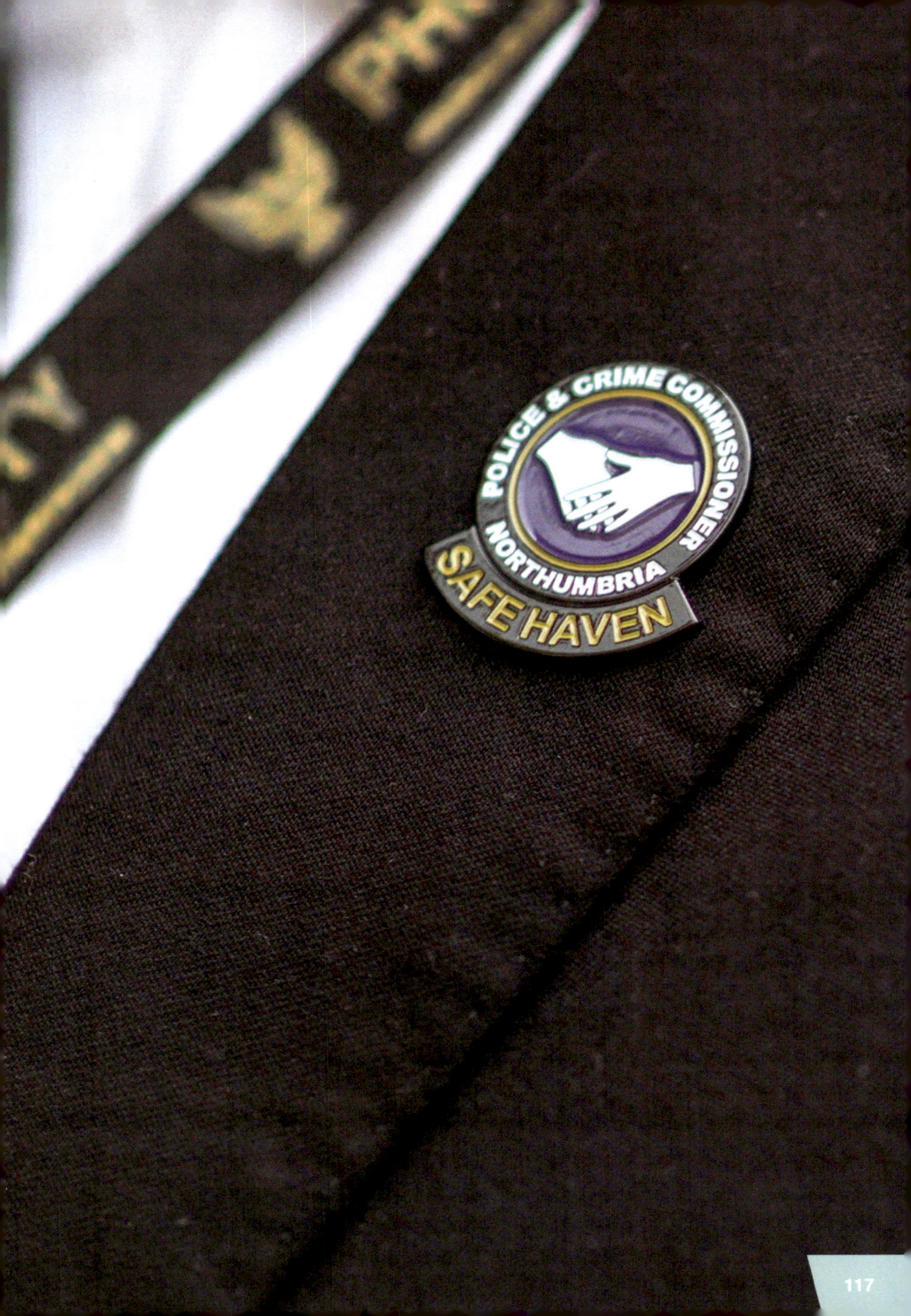
POLICE & CRIME COMMISSIONER
NORTHUMBRIA
SAFE HAVEN

made the victim of other serious personal crimes can amount to inhuman and degrading treatment. That means that when the police apparently doubted what the court found was the women's 'credible arguable claim' and failed to follow up some obvious leads, they were in breach of their duty to protect that right for those women. Additionally, of course, they left Worboys free to attack up to an estimated 195 other women and inflict inhuman and degrading treatment on them, before he was finally arrested.

This judgment is powerful. It will help abuse victims in Rotherham whose complaints were similarly neglected. In Northumbria Police it played a key role in the establishment of Operation Crystal, to re-investigate rape cases and the behaviour of officers who had categorised many of them as being 'no-crime' and set them aside. There must be a coincident risk that investigating, supervising and command rank officers can all be subject to criminal prosecution for misconduct in a public office by wilfully neglecting the duty to investigate serious offences, now that is shown to be a breach of the victims Article 3 rights. 'No-criming' credible claims of rape would be a clear example of failing to investigate.

Of course, the presence of these rights in national law has improved performance in public authorities and given thousands of people a tool to argue for better and fairer public services, without ever needing to go to court.

Some of the myths that have been propagated to discredit the Human Rights Act are easily countered.

In 2006 it was reported that police delivered a fried chicken dinner to a suspected car thief fleeing police and besieged on a roof 'because of his human rights'. Surprise, surprise, there is no human right to a KFC and the police were simply using a sensible tactic to help to negotiate him down.

Nor is there a bar to deporting a foreign criminal because he has a British cat, as Theresa May once claimed. Foreign criminals have tried to rely on the right to family life to argue that they should not be separated from loved ones who are in the UK but the courts can and do interfere with that right in the public interest. Whether a foreign criminal stays or goes requires a balancing of interests, unlikely to be greatly affected by having a cat.

Only slightly more complicated to unravel are other controversial cases. In January 2012, an appeal to the Strasbourg Court blocked our deportation of the radical Muslim cleric, Abu Qatada. Why should the UK be prevented from ridding itself of this dangerous man? That ruling was not about protecting his family life but because of well-evidenced fears that he would be tortured in his home country, at a time when an eight year legal battle had found him not guilty of any terrorist offences here. The practical outcome was that the Home Secretary agreed a new treaty with Jordan, guaranteeing Abu Qatada his right to a fair trial and he was deported in July 2013.

The most contested issue relates to the Strasbourg Court determining that some prisoners in British prisons for a short term should, like prisoners elsewhere in Europe, be allowed to vote. The litigating prisoner lost throughout our court hierarchy and won in Strasbourg. However, prior to the passage of the Act he would just have gone directly to Strasbourg with presumably the same outcome causing the same 'constitutional crisis'. The Government says that the Act undermines the role of UK courts and the sovereignty of Parliament. It does not do the former because the judgments of the Strasbourg Court of Human Rights are to 'have regard to'. They are not binding. The UK courts are the final arbiters of what our law, including human rights law, provides. Neither does the European Court clash with Parliamentary sovereignty. All it can do is determine whether there is a breach of the Convention, and if there is, it is for the UK Parliament to decide how to remedy the breach. The House of Commons passed a resolution refusing to enact new law. The judgment, which happened in 2005, has not been implemented and prisoners still do not vote in British prisons.

Repealing the Act, the Government's aim, would simply turn back the clock by making Strasbourg the only enforcement court again. Nothing else would go into reverse. The Convention Rights have underpinned our legal system since we signed up in 1951 and our courts have been directly implementing them now for the 15 years since the Human Rights Act so they are completely mixed into our common law now, like two very similar colours of paint.

David Cameron is said to have tasked Michael Gove with repealing the Human Rights Act and introducing a 'British Bill of Rights' in some way to better protect our home-grown values. However, our current human rights are our home grown values. They are those in the European Convention negotiated in 1951 and mainly designed by the British. Few people, even though they know little of the legal framework, would think that we should replace them with something different, the right to life, the right to freedom from torture, the right to a fair trial, to free association and the right to have a family. Repealing and replacing is also, as the former Tory Attorney General Dominic Grieve has said, 'legally illiterate' because our current rights are the ones in the Convention and we cannot reduce them unless we leave the 47 seat Council of Europe (which oversees the Convention). If the Human Rights Act was repealed and replaced by a British Bill of Rights, our membership of the Council means that all the Convention rights would stay a part of British law but we would have to go back to Strasbourg to enforce them.

The former Secretary of State for Justice, Chris Grayling went further and raised the possibility of leaving the Council of Europe to avoid the jurisdiction of the Strasbourg Court entirely. Leaving the Council would be the only way in which the Convention rights could be avoided. He suggested that the other 46 members should agree that, solely in the case of the UK, the Strasbourg Court should be reduced to an advisory role without even the need for regard for its judgments.

Here the issue becomes not only a legal mess but a wide ranging moral one. No other modern democracy has abandoned the principle of international human rights. They are signed up to in order to protect people from the excesses or failings of national government. Not surprisingly Britain has a good human rights record. Only 0.7% of the cases taken against the UK go to Strasbourg and succeed. But we are not a perfect rights-respecting democracy. The right for gay people to serve in the military; for male widowers to get a widow's pension and for the abolition of the fixed retirement age at 65 were all brought about or influenced by proceedings at the Strasbourg Court, sometimes against the wishes of our Government, in favour of ordinary people. This brings us back again to the point. human rights do not, as some newspapers suggest, favour the bad against the good. They help ordinary people. It is clear that when David Cameron talks about 'British human rights' he means 'the British Government's view of human rights'. What exactly would they be? Presumably not available for unpopular foreigners or prisoners. Would they apply to people on benefits? It would be a terrible example to other countries in the world, where people still have to fight for the rights we enjoy today.

If the UK Government could decide what human rights to have or remove, it would empower other regimes around the world to dilute their human rights protections when they become inconvenient.

Human rights are essential for ordinary people against just such a stance. No wonder this elitist Tory Government wants rid of them.

"That is a further point, extremely important for Northumbria. Crime levels and policing need are both significantly higher in our relatively poor area, especially in parts of the majority urban areas like inner city Sunderland which are very deprived."

13
FIGHTING FOR FAIR FUNDING FROM GOVERNMENT

Mrs Brown aged 94 and living alone was unsettled when she started to get silent phone calls. Her daughter, living far away, was concerned that the worry would damage her mother's health. She called Northumbria Police to ask their advice.

A neighbourhood PC and a Police and Community Support Officer called round just to say hello and Mrs Brown is now reassured that she has their number and can call Geoff or Pauline anytime if the calls come again or if anything else is scaring her.

Geoff, Pauline and hundreds of others are part of the local community police teams that the Chief Constable, like his colleagues in other metropolitan forces, is struggling to keep in place amidst 26% cuts to police budgets with another 25% threatened in the next five years. There seems to be no value attached to work such as that with Mrs Brown. The Government's oft repeated view is that the sole purpose of the police is to cut crime and since crime is going down they can continue to cut police forces too.

This is a fiction. Only 22% of officers' time is spent on crime. In Northumbria Police, almost a fifth of calls are about anti-social behaviour which is going up by 1300 incidents a year. Over half of calls are about public safety and welfare. 23 a day relate to missing persons (up 47% on 2009-10) 30 to incidents concerning mental health, there are

82 domestic abuse reports, most of which do not turn into crimes and, last year, there were almost 2000 times in our area, when police had to help out with ambulance calls.

Demand for policing nationwide has been analysed by The College of Policing. It found that a typical force will additionally, every day, manage 1700 dangerous offenders in the community on Multi-Agency Public Protection Arrangements (up by 31% since 2009-10), 1000 children on Child Protection Plans, 2000 families involved in Troubled Families Projects and chair 1200 Multi-Agency Risk Assessment Conferences keeping high risk domestic abuse victims safe. Then there are increasing intelligence reports about the terrorism threat to attend to and considerable 'service drift' as cuts force the ending of local authority services like noise abatement and police become the agency of last resort.

Even the Government's core argument that crime is going down is wrong. After two decades of decline across Europe, crime began to turn up last year in the UK. On 4th June this year, The National Audit Office reported that:

'Recorded crime increased by 2% between the years ending 2013 and 2014' *Financial sustainability of police forces in England and Wales:HC78 Session 2015-16 www.publications.parliament.uk/pa/cm201516/cmselect/cmpubacc/288/288.pdf*. The last quarter's figures show recorded sex crime up by 32%, rape by 40% and violence against the person by 21%. A recent House of Commons library report showed reported child sex abuse up 60% in four years.

The Tories rely on the Crime Survey for England and Wales which reported 11% fewer offences last year but the Crime Survey for England and Wales does not count homicide, sexual offences, people trafficking, cybercrime, fraud, forced marriage or honour-based crimes. Since it is a survey of what crime families have suffered in the period, shoplifting, petrol bilking, metal theft and other kinds of business crime are not counted either and it doesn't count 'victimless' crimes like possessing drugs. 31% of crime types - almost a third - is not counted by the Crime Survey for England and Wales *www.ons.gov.uk/ons/rel/crime-stats/crime-statistics/year-ending-september-2014/sty-stock-take-of-crime-statistics.html* As Professor Tim Hope said in a recent article for the Centre for Crime and Justice Studies:

"The Crime Survey for England and Wales is much better at not

measuring crime than it is at measuring crime's true extent"
www.crimeandjustice.org.uk/ resources/we-need-a-different- crime-survey.'

The Crime Survey for England and Wales is likely to start to record cyber-crime in the near future.

Since 2010, government funding to police forces has been slashed by a quarter. A recent report by the National Audit Office makes clear that Northumbria Police has, through this, lost the most cash of all the English police forces. It has lost 23% of its budget, which has caused the loss of 15% of its police officers and 37% of its staff.

We are the hardest hit because the vast bulk of our police funding comes from the government grant. There are different proportions in each police force. The other source of funding for police is that part of the local council tax which is a precept for policing. For historic reasons, largely because major parts of our area are poor, with high levels of unemployment and deprivation, the police precept is tiny in Northumbria, the smallest sum in the country. A band D property in our area will bring in £88.33 per year for policing and many properties in our poorer urban areas are only band A so that the actual cash produced is small.

In contrast, affluent Surrey has seen only a 12% funding cut to its overall police funding despite the 25% cut to the government grant because their police precept is much higher. A Band D property in Surrey will bring in a sum in the region of £200 but many houses will bring in more. Percentage cuts to the government grant therefore impact relatively lightly in affluent areas where the council tax take is higher. They unfairly discriminate against poorer areas but a straight percentage cut to the government grants discriminates particularly against Northumbria.

The Government indicates that in the impending Comprehensive Spending Review they intend to cut a further 25%-40% from the police grant nationwide by 2020. If they do not change the basis on which those cuts are distributed away from the same percentage across all forces, Northumbria will by 2020 have lost literally one half of its cash between 2010 and 2020 whilst Surrey will only have lost one quarter.

Despite the depth of these cuts Northumbria has retained neighbourhood policing as a priority whilst managing also to keep its Protecting Vulnerable Persons Unit strong. That is where

Police & Crime Commissioner for Northumbria
Vera Baird

announces Northumbria Police is now a Living Wage employer

We are a Living Wage Employer

VERA BAIRD QC
POLICE & CRIME COMMISSIONER

NORTHUMBRIA POLICE

victims of rape, child sexual exploitation, domestic abuse and similar crimes are safeguarded and those offences investigated. Like other forces we have cut middle management, reduced the number of area commands and sold off police stations, replacing them with rented shops, rooms in fire and rescue stations or other cheaper premises, sometimes bringing police more closely into the heart of our communities and turning a bad development into a good one.

79% of spending on policing is spent on people, the workforce which the public is keen to see retained and on its streets, boosting community confidence and preventing anti-social behaviour and crime. In common with many other forces Northumbria has now virtually exhausted all other possible savings and expects to lose, next year alone, more than 200 officers and between 200 and 300 civilian staff. In five years' time, Northumbria Police is likely to have fewer than 2500 officers instead of the current 3600.

Presumably Theresa May would regard this with equanimity, as long as the Crime Survey for England and Wales continues to be her only thermometer, but the recent National Audit Office Report ought to make her think again.

One of that reports' most significant findings refers to that error of simplicity in equating 'falling crime' with the ability to cut more police and points to the lack of information to justify the Home Office in driving cuts more deeply and its utter failure to understand the real demand on police forces. The report says:

"The Home Office has insufficient information to determine how much further it can reduce funding (for policing) without degrading services or when it may need to support individual forces… there is insufficient information to identify signs of the sector being unable to deliver services, unclear links between financial reductions and service pressures".

This makes clear that the Government is wrong to be sanguine about cutting funds on the basis of an arbitrary count of some crimes and that there is insufficient understanding of demand let alone an appreciation of when, in a specific force, such as Northumbria, the tipping point will come and bring a significant threat to community safety. A further aspect of risk is that the further predicted cuts of between 25% and 40% can be expected to be phased across a three year spending period, usually with the highest cuts loaded at the front. This means they will impact especially on workforce losses, long before successive years' crime statistics tell us whether crime is going up or down. Even on Theresa May's basis of working that means that there is a risk that the imminent cuts will force us to be cutting officers as crime goes up.

The National Audit Office also noted that:

"The Department's current funding approach does not consider the circumstance of individual forces. Since 2011-12 the Department has applied the same percentage funding reduction to all forces. The current funding approach does not consider the full range of demands on police time, relative efficiency or the split between central and local funding on individual forces".

That is a further point, extremely important for Northumbria. Crime levels and policing need are both significantly higher in our relatively poor area, especially in parts of the majority urban areas like inner city Sunderland which are very deprived. Compare and contrast the position of Surrey again where the Police and Crime Commissioner complains that there is nonetheless a risk to his population's well-being from further cuts, although his cuts to date have been far less and his area lacks some of the criminogenic factors present here.

There is yet a further point to show the weakness of the cut-crime-cut-police argument, demonstrated by reference to Northumbria's Project Sanctuary, a strategy to unearth and tackle organised and semi-organised sexual exploitation of the vulnerable. It compromises undercover work and covert surveillance to infiltrate current networks of abuse and a vast marketing programme by the neighbourhood teams, taking awareness of the signs of abuse out to the public so that they can act as further eyes and ears. In its original form Sanctuary required more than 40 senior police officers dedicated to it for 18 months with the neighbourhood teams in the appropriate localities also dedicated solely to this work and not deployed on other community-based work and in addition to the involvement of specialist covert resources from time to time. Police, working with partners, have uncovered and charged over 120 rapes or related crimes, involving large numbers of vulnerable people who must be safeguarded and sustained as potential witnesses by police in addition to core officer tasks of detection and investigation.

The cost in police officer hours and expertise has been enormous, clearly a far higher cost and application of resource than that required to detect and charge 103 'traditional' crimes such as those the Crime Survey for England and Wales counts like criminal damage and burglary. That shows a further flaw in the Government's logic of attaching funding to numbers of crimes. 'Traditional' crimes cost far less and it is those crimes which are continuing to decline whilst reports of sexual exploitation of the vulnerable and historic sexual abuse are steeply increasing. To use an old phrase counting them together is not counting apples with apples and being so much more complex, sensitive and time consuming, policing of abuse cases needs to be counted in a different way.

The sworn duties of a constable under the Crown, require them to be responsible for the protection of life and property, maintenance of order, prevention and detection of crime and prosecution of offenders against the peace. We need therefore to make clear that when the Tories suggest that crime is diminishing and police are less needed, it is untrue. Any more cuts risk leaving our most vulnerable to live with abuse without help and the thousands of members of the public who seek police support without anyone to aid them.

14 THE ROLE OF THE POLICE
   AND CRIME COMMISSIONER

SECTION
3

THE ROLE OF THE POLICE AND CRIME COMMISSIONER

"After three years of work as the Police and Crime Commissioner for Northumbria I have stuck to the principles and practices set out in my first year in Office."

14
THE ROLE OF THE POLICE AND CRIME COMMISSIONER

When I was elected as Northumbria's Police and Crime Commissioner in November 2012 the role was little valued and barely understood, and for a while all political parties were engaged in a debate about its future. Three years on, I am more positive than I was then because I have seen first-hand the difference that this new leadership role can make to local communities - but there is still a lot to consider.

On the first anniversary of our election, Theresa May, the Home Secretary, delivered a 'warts and all' assessment admitting disappointment at the low voter turnout nationally. (In Northumbria, turnout was low but above the national average and I won 56% of the poll outright in the first round, with 100,170 votes). Since then she has regularly quoted Police and Crime Commissioner achievements and grown strong in her support. Since then too, the Tories have given Police and Crime Commissioners responsibility for victim services and now have plans which might bring Fire and Rescue Services under their remit. Ms May has made clear that the bar is set high for any police boundary changes allowing incorporation of the Police and Crime Commissioner role into regional mayoralties. So the Government's commitment seems clear and, with Police and Crime Commissioner

Elections next May and again on General Election Day 2020, the role is likely to continue, in most places for most of the next decade.

The Labour Party has always opposed Police and Crime Commissioners, but early policy to replace them with a group of Local Authority Leaders changed as Labour Police and Crime Commissioners started to innovate and became more fully accepted locally. In an attempt to capture the authority of a single focus professional the Party advocated having a Chair for the Leaders' group, chosen from outside the local authorities - a role a little like that of the Police and Crime Commissioner. 'Letting in the Light' a Fabian pamphlet I edited with contributions from all 13 Labour Police and Crime Commissioners demonstrated our creativity, as pockets of real Labour Government, whilst the national Party was out of power.

The new Shadow Home Secretary, Andy Burnham, who met with us at Labour Party Conference to gain closer knowledge of how the role works, is now reconciled to its retention and open to joint policy development and joint campaigning against government funding cuts.

Nonetheless, some myths still need busting. For example, there are no big savings to be gained from abolishing Police and Crime Commissioners, as previously suggested in Parliament; the only saving would have been from scrapping next year's election. Indeed the Taxpayers Alliance has recently confirmed that Police and Crime Commissioners are actually £2m a year cheaper, nationally, than the Police Authorities they replaced. In this area alone I have saved £2,912m, the highest saving in the country, cutting 68% off the cost of the former Northumbria Police Authority and investing it all into policing and community safety.

Police and Crime Commissioners are also not an add-on which could be scrapped and the money put into frontline policing, as is sometimes suggested, unless the idea is to scrap all public governance over the police. Although local police services are generally popular with the public, we are all aware of the high profile cases of national concern like Hillsborough, Orgreave, the Steven Lawrence investigation and, more recently, the killings of Jean Charles De Menezes and Mark Duggan and the appalling decision to allow undercover officers to have affairs with female climate campaigners whilst collecting evidence on their political activities. Police have huge powers over the public and have to be their servants, not their

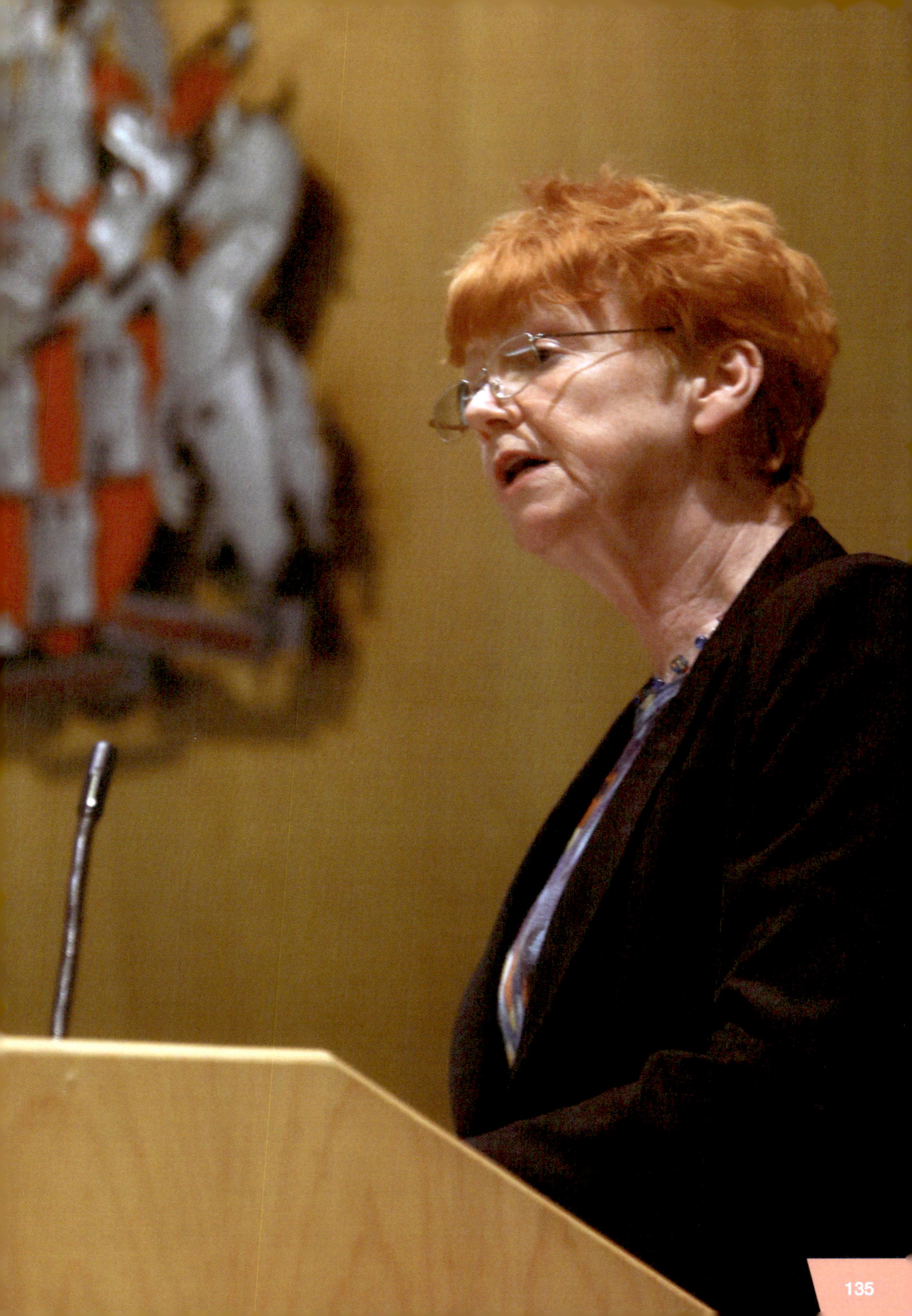

masters. Electing a Commissioner who controls the police budget and can dismiss the Chief Constable is extremely important in this context; representing a significant shift of power from the police to the public, whom they are meant to serve.

In England and Wales there has always been elected police governance, though not until now directly elected. Police Authorities preceded Police and Crime Commissioners and they were made up of Councillors, seconded from each of the local authorities in the policing area, together with some Magistrates and a group of 'independents', essentially chosen by the other members.

In terms of direct costs, although it is no criticism of the former membership of Northumbria Police Authority, the allowances for such a large group attending numerous meetings came to more than the cost of my salary and that of the Deputy Commissioner I took on for the first year after my election. Additionally, there was some truth in what Theresa May said, when opening the House of Commons Second Reading debate on the Police Reform and Social Responsibility Bill in 2011:

"Although giving strategic direction and obtaining value for money are their two main functions, Police Authorities have neither the democratic mandate to set police priorities nor the capability to scrutinise police performance nor are they properly accountable themselves".

At that time too, surveys showed that two thirds of the public wanted more influence on how the police were serving them and only 7% of people had ever heard of Police Authorities. It was Labour, not the Tories, who first proposed elections. Both David Blunkett and Jacqui Smith, when each was Home Secretary, tried for direct democracy either for Police Authorities as a whole or for their Chairs. Both understood that democratic government over policing is vital.

Less of a myth and more of an easy misunderstanding is, I suspect, that both many fellow politicians and the wider public haven't appreciated that the role of Police and Crime Commissioner is an executive one. It is almost unique in Britain to have such an elected executive person. My impression in many conversations is that people think there is just me, in the same way that there is just one person who is the local MP, with a very small team to do back-up administration and not much else.

For example, one of the former candidates against me in the election, famously said on local radio on its first anniversary that if he were Police and Crime Commissioner he would not have 'an expensive team'; there would just be him. I could only wish him luck. Firstly, the statute compels every Police and Crime Commissioner to have a Chief Executive and a Chief Finance Officer, very sensibly since the Commissioner must set the force budget and monitor expenditure ensuring value for money for local communities. They must also determine the Policing Precept for the area and scrutinise efficiency and effectiveness. Northumbria's budget is much depleted through government cuts, but it is nonetheless £270m of public funds in 2015-16, and we have to make best use of and account for every penny. This requires careful budgeting, scrutiny, accounting, audit, and investment management.

The Police Reform and Social Responsibility Act 2012 also requires Police and Crime Commissioners to secure and maintain the police force for their area by setting the police and crime priorities, including direct engagement with local communities to ensure their needs are met. We must put all that into a 5 year Police and Crime Plan, publish Annual Reports and answer bi-monthly to the local Police and Crime Panel. I appoint the Chief Constable, hold him to account for running the force and, if necessary, dismiss him. Holding the force to account through the Chief Constable requires ensuring that the force contributes to the national and international policing capabilities set out by the Home Secretary as well as working fully on local policing. It requires compliance with all the equality and diversity duties, and makes me responsible for ensuring (through the Chief Constable) the safeguarding of children and the promotion of child welfare. I must also oversee and scrutinise how complaints against the police are managed.

In addition there are further statutory obligations on every Police and Crime Commissioner relating to the 'and Crime' aspect of the role; where the range of responsibilities and the reach are even wider. We must work with fire and rescue services, local authorities, directors of public health and clinical commissioning groups to improve the safety of our communities. Similarly, we must also work with the courts, probation services, youth offending teams, prisons and the Crown Prosecution Service to ensure the efficiency and effectiveness of the wider Criminal Justice System and to inform our delivery of what is now ninety percent of all victim support services.

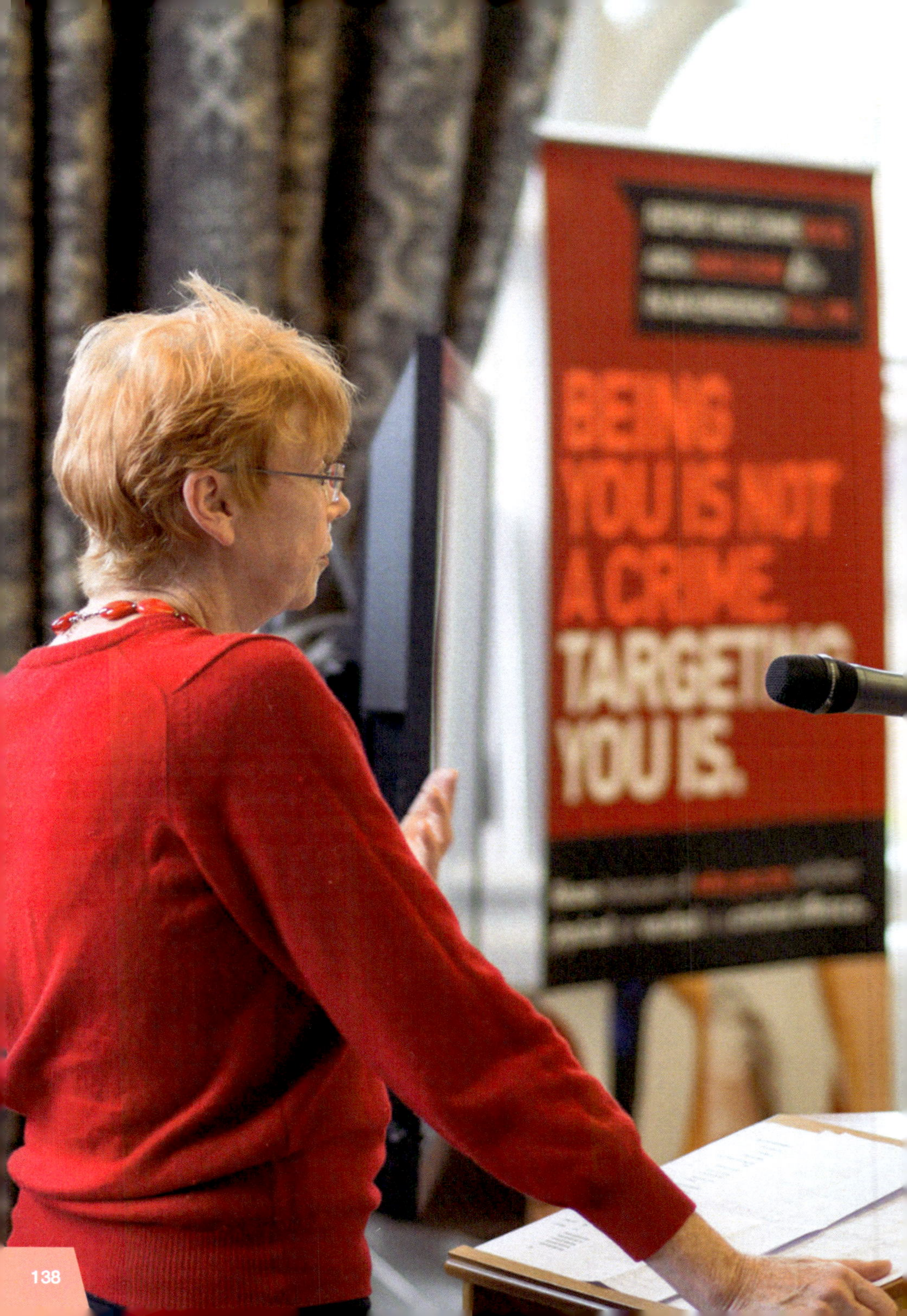
BEING
YOU IS NOT
A CRIME
YOU IS.

Since last April, Commissioners have, additionally had full responsibility for delivering support to victims, save for a few specific services which are still nationally commissioned. This is a huge addition to our role, which has involved commissioning a core service in close liaison with the police, for when they are involved, but also establishing clear accessibility for victims of crime who require help but do not want to be in contact with the police. To ensure that everyone is helped to cope with and recover from what has happened to them, Police and Crime Commissioners also have to commission specialist local support services and to make arrangements to recruit and manage local volunteers.

We have additionally been given the role of implementing restorative justice wherever it can be made available to a victim and where it might also have a beneficial impact on the offender. Many of us see Restorative Justice - which has long been in the lexicon of justice measures but has been indifferently implemented - as an important potential tool for improving victim satisfaction and recovery. However it does require extremely careful and effective management.

These are all inescapable obligations and do not start to cover the many other activities we undertake in the public interest such as responding to national consultations, shaping public policy through the Association of Police and Crime Commissioners or attending Home Office, Ministry of Justice and other departmental discussions and conferences often several times a month.

It is possible that some resistance to Police and Crime Commissioners came from the misunderstanding that it is 'just one person' scrutinising a huge police force. It is more like being the hands-on Chair of a company board or the Chief Executive of a trade union.

The Commons Home Affairs Committee Inquiry in December 2014 into the election of the 41 elected Commissioners (13 of whom are Labour) found that reforms were needed to ensure the new system did not put at further risk public trust in the police. The appointment of 'crony' deputies was much criticised, for example, but that has no application to Northumbria. My Deputy for one year was a much respected former senior police officer who was of immense help in identifying the most appropriate routes by which to apply effective scrutiny so that the force is held fully to account for the public.

The committee struck a positive note in saying that the new Commissioners have provided greater clarity of leadership for policing within their areas and that we are increasingly recognised by the public as accountable for the strategic direction of their police forces. Their report goes on to say:

"It is still too early to determine whether the introduction of Police and Crime Commissioners has been a success. Indeed, even by 2016, it may be difficult to draw a national picture because of the range of different approaches being taken by Commissioners."

There certainly are different approaches to the role. However, both in this region and nationally, Labour Police and Crime Commissioners have used the power entrusted to us to develop better partnership models of crime prevention and control to enhance community safety and to improve the Criminal Justice System. In addition we have used it to showcase ethical Labour policies, such as becoming living wage employers, recruiting modern apprentices and procuring goods and services competitively but principally from the public sector.

I set out to put victims first, tackle domestic and sexual abuse, cut crime, deal with anti-social behaviour, and build community confidence in the police, and that work is well under way.

Labour in opposition developed its own policies to raise supplementary police funding but they are relatively small scale and no substitute for government reconsidering its current intention to implement further cuts.

Local income can be earned from offering 'speed awareness courses' for people convicted of minor speeding offences. They spread positive learning, limit penalty points to higher speeds and, importantly, are paid directly to local police, whereas fines go to the exchequer. Similarly, an alcohol behaviour course, implemented in Northumbria as an alternative to a penalty notice for being drunk and disorderly, returns some of the cost of policing to the local community whilst teaching people how better to manage alcohol in future. Forces that have to clear up after high profile football matches and profitable night-time concerts will soon be looking for better recompense from the private sector. There are also attempts to increase police funding by returning a fairer share of the proceeds of crime to the communities who suffered from the offences.

However, there is still a need to do more for less, pointing towards expanding partnership sources of crime reduction to support neighbourhood policing. These small teams of police officers, dedicated to policing a certain community, are the bedrock of modern policing delivery and were well defined as occupying the 'social role of policing' in Lord Stevens' Independent Police Commission report of November 2013. Officers and Community Support Officers on the ground are working with the public and with partners to solve problems together by early intervention and by finding longer term solutions to any wider threats to stability and community safety.

The effect of neighbourhood policing has not only been overwhelmingly positive for communities, it has also helped to model a new kind of police officer. Often remote from hierarchical management, they are accountable to the local communities they serve and work on the frontline exercising initiative and discretion. Because they are loyal to the public as well as to the police force, the trust they evoke contrasts with the distrust with which the national policing hierarchy is often still regarded. Their role also makes them subject to day to day scrutiny by the local public, whilst at the other end of the police force hierarchy, there is now intrusive scrutiny by an elected Police and Crime Commissioner. These multi-level inter-relationships with others will make it harder in future for the police to act as it has at times in the past, as a self-serving institution favouring its own interests over those of the public.

Devolution proposals, consideration of merging blue light services and ever deeper cuts to funding are all emerging features of the changing police, justice and political landscape that Police and Crime Commissioners occupy. In a time of upheaval as well as innovation, Labour Police and Crime Commissioners are continuing to navigate pathways to protect the high levels of community safety and low crime which our local communities currently enjoy and to engage as many people as possible in supporting our hard pressed police. In Northumbria we have been at the forefront of such innovation. We intend to continue in the same vein.